3/2017
To Josh & Molly—
  Thanks for being.

MW01613100

LOST&FOUND

CARRIE BULLOCK FISHER

LOST&
FOUND
A Journey of Faith

Published by Looking Glass Stories

http://lookingglassstories.com

ISBN 978-0-9883622-1-5

Cover Image: Boy at Sea by Georgia Fisher

Cover Design by Joey Hayes

To all who have blessed my life with relationship, you've given me the opportunity to learn about the hearts of God, myself, and others. At times the lessons have been painful; at times, my ability to love well has been exposed as grossly inadequate, but these lessons have not been in vain.

For Dean C., Andrew V.C., Levi C., Steven G., Richard S., Kenyon C., David S., Tully B., and Joe F., extraordinary individuals making their way as best they can in a difficult world. Their gentle spirits, tender hearts, and boundless courage are worthy gifts to all who choose to know them.

ACKNOWLEDGEMENTS

What started as something that felt like an isolated journey has become a picture of God's provision, of His ability to open doors and of His reminder that we are never alone.

Brian, Joe, and Georgia, thank you for your encouragement, and Brian, for your technical support.

Joey, you're a friend for life! For all your help, I can never thank you enough.

Little Bob, my beloved brother, your willingness to fill in the gaps of my memories was most helpful.

To Rebel, Mary E. and Charles, you graciously offered your home to someone you hadn't seen in thirty years, allowing me to write in peace. What an incredible gesture of love.

To my dear friends who offered help along the way, thank you for accompanying me in this journey. I have benefited from the generosity of your friendship.

CONTENTS

Part II: The Least of These

Part III: A Window to the Soul

INTRODUCTION

Was it happenstance or some sort of fore-shadowing? Whatever it was, it was hard to ignore. Five lanes of traffic were reduced to a crawl along the interstate long after the morning rush hour should've cleared. Reaching the source of the obstruction, I saw a jackknifed tractor-trailer stretching across the entire westbound side of the interstate.

Once past this obstacle, cars began picking up speed. However, just a short distance later, traffic again came to a standstill. Realizing this was going to be an even longer wait, I shut off my SUV's engine. A helicopter arrived on the scene and hovered overhead; I wondered if it was preparing to transport someone in need of medical attention.

Eventually a few of us ventured out of our vehicles. This morning trek into town had become a two-hour delay and counting. Conversation between some of the bystanders was about how the holdup would affect their day. We were all late--for work or appointments--and many were feeling the burden of falling behind before the day even started.

I couldn't shake the feeling, however, that this holdup was more than a nuisance to some of these by-standers. With the aid of my smart-phone, I was able to confirm my suspicions: this second tie-up involved a fatality.

Behind us, emergency workers closed the interstate to all westbound traffic. We travelers beyond the barricade were eventually allowed to creep past what had now become a full scale investigation. We were directed to drive as far on the shoulder as we could safely pass, so as not to disturb the scene. Being one of the first to drive past the carnage, I couldn't help but venture a look at six vehicles bearing the marks of a disastrous collision.

One car in particular stood out. It was a blue sedan sitting ominously alone and facing backwards on the road. It was almost completely crumpled. Draped over what had once been the driver's seat was a deflated, bright yellow air-bag. The sight took my breath away, reminding me how fleeting life can be. It was also a reminder that in life, one man's devastation is often merely a curiosity, or worse yet an inconvenience, to others. An uncomfortable pang welled up within me at this feeling of disconnectedness.

My own agenda for the day had to be modified because of the delay. Grocery shopping for my son would need to be rescheduled. I'd be able to make the breakfast appointment he'd begged me for, since my daughter, a few miles away at her on-campus apartment, agreed to pick her non-driving brother up. This was a big help since I was running so late.

After our rushed breakfast, I drove my son to the doctor. Still mindful of the circumstances surrounding the drive into town, I felt as though a dark cloud had settled around me. However, while patient and doctor met for a brief time, I needed to focus on the task at hand: preparing for what I feared would be a showdown with this physician. I felt the course of treatment he'd chosen for my son's illness wasn't effective. I'd hoped for more, some measure of hope that things would get easier.

What I didn't expect was for this trusted man, who'd worked side by side with us for over eight years, to suggest we may be losing the battle. Yet that's exactly what he did, as he matter-of-factly explained the illness may be progressing, that what quality of life we struggled to hold onto for my son may in fact be slipping through my grasping fingers. And there was that feeling again, the same one I'd been reminded of on my drive into town.

My son's life was hanging in the balance, yet duty called. The doctor had patients to see, opinions to give, and prescriptions to write. I sensed it was time for me to go so he could get on with his day. I'd have to process this disheartening news on my own.

Leaving the doctor's office, I was shaken. I didn't want to consider the possibility that my first-born's condition might be worsening. Yet this wasn't my first encounter with suffering. Pain and disappointment have made appearances in my life a number of times over the years, all the way back to when I was a mere child armed with nothing more than a heart full of longing to be loved and accepted. I didn't realize then that my desire for these things reflected the relationships I had with myself, my family and most importantly, my God.

The faith from my childhood that would influence my life and my relationships for years to come was more of a superficial, idealistic notion that wasn't all that helpful. Along the way, I came to believe the religious messages I was all too familiar with were of little use to me. In fact, in many instances, it seemed the messages were of little use to the individuals advocating them as well!

Thankfully, I've learned suffering and pain can do more than overwhelm. These became powerful forces in my life that ultimately set me on a journey for answers to the questions my soul longed to discover and know. Was I truly alone? Was there more to hope for than the preservation of life as I knew it? For my life seemed to be paved with so much disconnection, so many broken relationships, and ultimately, so much pain.

Sometimes to find the light we must look beyond the shadows that may distract or discourage us. As I searched for a way out of the brokenness that had, over time, gained such a grip on me, I began to examine my misconstrued notions about God, His relationship to me and my relationship to others. In the process, I discovered Someone who's moved by the difficulties of my life, Someone who offers purpose for my existence; Someone who inspires hope even in the midst of pain; and Someone who calls His people into ever-deepening relationship.

We're all on a journey. And there's no denying that many of the travelers we encounter along the way are dealing with their own wrong turns, dead ends, and wreckage. Some are desperate to know they aren't alone and uncared for, and that there is salvation from the suffering and chaos of their lives.

Then there is our faith journey. Sadly, those who are religious are often faith's worst ambassadors! There is hope for those struggling to survive difficult circumstances and whose hearts feel abandoned. There is healing for those who've been wounded or alienated by blows of an unseen enemy. Being able to communicate this greater reality starts with you and me allowing God to guide us into an honest look at our own faith, allowing Him to shine His light into the shadows of our own hearts, and allowing His Spirit to expose the motivations that influence our own actions.

It's time for us to examine the quality of our relationships and our faith; for the temptation isn't unlike that of my fellow-commuters' that morning on the interstate: becoming too focused on our own agendas. Through my son's illness, God has chosen to lead me into a valley of suffering where many struggle to hold on. In this place, the message of the Gospel often rings hollow to those who hear it. We who have the privilege of bearing God's good news desperately need to discover how this could be.

If we as brothers and sisters in the faith are going to bridge a growing crisis of disconnectedness, we must be willing to consider our brokenness and our constant need of rescue from our limitations and downfalls. We must be willing to understand that very often, we are the victims in need of rescue, no matter how strong our spiritual convictions.

I'll admit, such vulnerability may not sound appealing in today's culture. It's tempting to keep forging ahead while maintaining a positive outlook, right? Because, what if? What if our brokenness overwhelms us? What if change doesn't seem possible? What if we sacrifice the things we've come to count on for comfort in this life? What if we lose control? Or what if we simply don't know how?

These were some of the challenges I faced in my struggle. They're stumbling blocks to our ability to live free, to the quality of our relationships, and in the purity of our faith-- until we're willing to fight our way through them.

I come as one who's struggled in my own journey of life and faith and who finally chose to arise from that place of isolation. I've discovered the Lord God is worth finding in the darkest corners of our broken hearts and in the deepest longing of our devoted lives. For when our worlds fall apart, He will not fail us. When devastation comes, He will not disappoint. When rejection brings its bitter sting, He offers His unending presence. He is worthy of becoming known, even in these places.

Only God can find the lost and bind the broken. I know because I was lost and broken; now I'm finding myself restored, in Him.

PART I

LIVING IN THE LAND OF THE LOST

My beautiful child, My joy!
I've created you to know a magnificent love.
As you discover the depth and wonder of My love,
You'll grow to flourish in all I've given.
You'll be free to love those around you,
And love in ways unique to you.
It's for this purpose I've made you.
You were born into the world at this time
And this place according to My plan.
Though I've made you in My image,
You're not yet complete.
You'll know loss and disappointment.
You'll struggle mightily because of your sin
And the ill-effects of the sins of others.
But it's these very things that will move you
To search for Me. In finding Me,
You'll overcome and be made complete.
In the world, you may feel small. But I'll take
What seems miniscule and make something
Of unimaginable worth. Your heart will be glad,
And My glory will be revealed in you.

-CARRIE BULLOCK FISHER

The Examiner *January 19, 1969*

LOCAL CHILD DISAPPEARS WHILE ON FISHING EXPEDITION

By CARRIE BULLOCK FISHER

A LOCAL CHILD IS THOUGHT TO BE missing in what is being described as a possible kidnapping. The disappearance seems to have occurred during a routine fishing trip. The exact time of the suspected abduction remains unknown.

Authorities were not initially notified since it appears no one noticed the child's absence until discovering several of the child's items abandoned along an unnamed county road. The child is thought to have been alone at the time of the incident.

Updates to this story will be made as details become available.

"For I know the plans I have for you," declares the LORD, "plans to prosper you and not to harm you, plans to give you hope and a future."

GOD (JEREMIAH 29:11)

There were no outward signs that would've set off alarms. No one suspected I was in distress. Yet the absence of glaring evidence only complicated my situation. I was a little girl whose heart wandered off in search of something, or perhaps to hide from something; perhaps it was some of both. With a heart set on wandering, young and naïve as I was, trouble was bound to come.

I'd spend decades of my life feeling lost and disconnected without understanding what precisely was lost or how to reclaim what was missing from my life. I'd also eventually realize I had a life-threatening enemy, whose dedicated efforts to snatch away my very life were far more sophisticated and discreet than I could've imagined.

Growing up in a Christian home in the religious safety of the Bible Belt, I wasn't lacking for access to the promises of God. Thanks to the dedication of faithful Sunday school teachers, I had ample opportunities to learn about these promises from an early age. However, it wasn't the foundation of a liberating salvation that settled into the depths of my understanding.

I was naïve, and possessed little understanding of the complex relationship of my mental, physical, and spiritual existence. I was clueless as to how to incorporate the Christian concepts and ideals I was learning about into my deeper existence. So before I understood how to fully embrace salvation, I'd already taken matters into my own hands. Faced with a growing emptiness, I settled for a limited and ultimately unsatisfying way of living, as I looked to fulfill my longings for love and significance.

Little did I know, I was forfeiting pieces of myself along the way. I aspired to make my life work and did it by attempting to manipulate my circumstances and often the people around me in my efforts to get my wants and needs met. It wasn't that I was a blatant manipulator; it's just that my motives were suspect. However, I grew quite adept at justifying my actions and thought processes as I fine-tuned the art of self-preservation.

The areas in my life where I found the affirmation I craved were innocent enough. I was the youngest child and only daughter in my family. This worked in my favor in earning attention from my dad; unfortunately, it came at the expense of my brother. Since I was a good student, I had no trouble winning my teachers' favor. And my family was well regarded in our community, which provided opportunities I might not have received otherwise. When all else failed, I learned to use humor, at my own expense if need be, to satisfy my longing for attention.

These behaviors don't seem particularly unusual or troublesome until one considers their potential for damage. I was attempting to get my needs met in devious ways that often came at my own expense or at the expense of others. As my childhood progressed, I was surviving, but I wasn't advancing. I wasn't learning to communicate honestly. I wasn't cultivating an ability to articulate my needs effectively.

I was further troubled by a perceived necessity of keeping up appearances. The weight of meeting the expectations I felt many had of me were also a burden. Though I wanted to please, there was a battle raging within me I didn't understand. In a convergence of spiritual, familial, and personal ambiguities, I felt misunderstood, unknown, and even unwanted.

Quite frankly, I lacked the wisdom and maturity to understand the depth and breadth of my need. As an uninformed and ill-equipped caretaker of my inner self, I was failing, feeling only emptiness, isolation, and ultimately, deep sadness. Survival for me meant casting about from the depths of my darkness and finding and relying on strategies that brought a kind of relief. But that relief was only temporary at best, and destructive at its worst.

As I reflect back on that time in my life, it's easy to recognize how lost and disconnected I felt, yet at the time, it was all I knew. While my inner self languished, I settled into a makeshift rhythm of living as a shell of who I was made to be. Though familiarity often breeds contempt, I've discovered familiarity also breeds acceptance, tolerance, and even respect. I tolerated life as I was experiencing it because it's what made sense to me. Any deviation of that would've struck my shallow reasoning as uncomfortable and therefore most certainly not worthwhile. So because of my familiarity with it, I became quite attached to this unsatisfactory way of living.

A long time ago, Jesus offered His disciples an incredible salvation, the restoration and preservation of the very lives they hungered for; the life I was hungering for. What was the story on these men who encountered Christ? How was it their lives changed so dramatically?

In the three years they spent with Jesus, the disciples laughed, cried, questioned and, more than anything, learned there was more to life, more to them, than they'd perceived. Yet in one calculated and cruel act, Jesus was gone, crucified; overcome, it seemed, by power-hungry men. The salvation and life they'd come to know? Surely it was forever beyond their reach.

With no sign of Jesus, I wonder if these disciples felt they even had a choice of what to do next. Had the Teacher's words been idealistic notions? Should these brothers and friends, who'd left behind lives of commercial fishing and debt collecting, be doomed to return to fish for their existence, instead of walking out the lives they glimpsed in their time with Him? And just like that, the enemy must surely have begun circling their vulnerable souls, as a vulture scouts its prey.

In their darkest moment, with hearts most likely full of doubt, confusion, and fear, something unimaginable happened; there was Jesus! Somehow, He was standing again in their midst. Though His followers had difficulty wrapping their minds around such a thing, He'd miraculously risen! Spending His last precious moments with them before ascending to the Father, Jesus looked into the eyes of these desperate men whom He'd called His friends. And then He did a perplexing thing. Scripture says He rebuked them for their lack of faith and for their stubborn refusal to believe.[1]

Honestly, I'm troubled by that holy rebuke. That Jesus would say such things at what had to be a vulnerable time to those who'd given up everything to follow Him causes me to wince, until I remind myself His motivation was love. If we'd been there to hear for ourselves, we'd know His tone held no trace of condemnation. His intent wasn't to shame. He confronted in love what their circumstances and instincts had reduced them to. In the midst of their attempt to survive the chaos, He knew the disciples' sacrifices, good intentions, and the very life they hoped for would be lost if they didn't walk in the faith they'd found in Him.

Of course, it's taken decades for me to gain such perspective. A love that exposes what is lost and wandering yet is safe isn't always an easy love to know or submit our hearts to. I'd merely been reacting to what I saw and heard in my own life. My faith was grounded in a wistful hope that everything would work itself out in the end. My perception of God grew out of my own jumbled feelings of narcissism and insignificance.

What great plans could the Father possibly have for me? As ashamed as I would've been to admit it, my relationship to God was filled with dread, fear, and the kind of loneliness that comes at the rejection of another when their love is desperately longed for.

Misperceptions and uncertainty, I've learned, shape how we submit our hearts and minds to a God whose intentions we aren't sure we trust. Though I hadn't walked beside Jesus as the disciples had, my life had been saturated with biblical instruction. I knew Him! At least I knew things about Him.

Yet somehow along the way, I failed to grasp an experiential knowledge of His love. I had no inkling of who I truly was or how to go about living out my faith. And I was at a loss for understanding how to submit my wounded heart and my deceived mind to this mysterious and invisible One for help in finding my way.

After a while, I grew weary from hoping I could do enough and be good enough to earn God's favor. I was terrified of being exposed for the pretender I was. I longed for meaning and truth and a love that was more powerful than the watered-down imitation I was acquainted with. My attempts at fishing for a satisfactory life led me to the same place the disciples found their faith, disoriented and in need of rescue.

This tendency to resort to our own devices to survive our circumstances isn't all that surprising. We're born into a fallen world in a vulnerable state. We have no clue of this enemy who actively works to skew our perception of God or the salvation made possible in Christ, no inkling that he seeks to deprive us of the very life God has provided. Fortunately, God waits with the patience of One who loves perfectly. But what's He waiting for? Is the burden on us to bring change or to be good enough? That was the question I couldn't answer.

Faced with the emptiness before me, my attention finally turned from self-preservation and fruitless 'works' in the name of Christ, to God, my Restorer. I began to realize God was waiting for me to trust Him and to yield my heart to His penetrating love so He could begin the work of redemption and restoration within my life. It was a sorely needed process. He began working His love and promises into the depths of my heart, as He did with His disciples so many years ago. I no longer had to settle for the faithlessness that had become such a limiting force in my life.

Like the disciples who found themselves, or at least their faith, wandering in the wake of Jesus' death, I've learned of modern-day wanderers, longing for something more than Christian clichés. People who find themselves lost and casting their own line, desperately fishing for something to hope for and believe in. I've seen the damage in and through well-meaning believers, who've become caught up in a world that's a busy jungle where only the strong survive; yet we weren't called to just survive. We've been invited into something far more glorious: to prosper in the journey of becoming. It's in becoming, that we discover true connectedness within the Body of Christ.

Our survival techniques and misguided fishing have netted too much loss and division within this Body. We, like the disciples so long ago, are desperate for our Restorer to shine His revealing light into our hearts. As we allow ourselves to be encouraged by the love of a God who is faithful, may He

- make us mindful of the strategies we rely on for comfort and survival,
- enable us to reach beyond our faithlessness,
- prod us to see beyond the partial truths that limit us, and
- open our eyes to discover the way to an unrealized destiny.

We're in need of the ongoing and transforming work of salvation. Without it, we're rendered ineffective in our search for life. Collectively, without this ongoing work, we're reduced to a shell of the Body, unable to care for its own. Our identity is in Christ. We know this. But how do we take hold of it? How do we discover and embrace this elusive existence in the midst of our own doubts, fears, and confusion?

What if the news suddenly broke that someone nearby was missing? Shock waves would most certainly reverberate at the realization that a crime has been committed so close to you. Becoming caught up in the urgency of the moment, what if you decided to join in the search for a life possibly hanging in the balance?

Your search team follows a trail of evidence leading you to a faraway place. But you're committed to the search now. You've decided life is more important, and there's no turning back. Left behind are the ever-present demands and restrictions of your normal reality. Unencumbered by the stresses of time, appearances and expectations, you unexpectedly feel a sense of freedom you didn't know existed.

You notice and approach a small group of men. They're sharing a meal together, yet their attention is fixed on one Man. In a cloud of confusion, you struggle to get your bearings, and it occurs to you that this Man is the newly risen Jesus. As the conversation unfolds, you realize you've somehow become an observer between Christ and His disciples as He prepares to ascend to the Father. You recall reading about this encounter. Straining to remember the details, you realize you're standing on Mt. Olivet.

But there's so much more to take in than a distant story. The disciples were obviously full of emotion. Elated at being reunited with this Man they love. Sadness at the betraying act of one of their own. Shame at their own failings. Fear of the unknown.

You're taken aback when you realize how much more real this encounter is than anything you imagined. It isn't just a conversation that occurred and was preserved for all of history. These were real men whose minds were confused, whose hearts were aching, and whose lives were at stake. It's in this place of desperation that Jesus opens His mouth to speak.

Your mind races back to the search that brought you here, the search for a missing person. Could it be the one who's missing is actually you? That, like me, in spite of your good intentions and most diligent efforts, you're not the glorious overcomer it seems you should be?

Or perhaps you seek the Body, the one commissioned to prepare the world to encounter Christ in the glorious reunion that's our destiny; brothers and sisters whose lives bear evidence of the effect of grace at work within their hearts.

Here in this place, I pray you'll see others gather to embark on this same journey. Together, as we seek Truth, may we hear words of life from Jesus.

There's safety in His presence, though we, like the disciples, may be filled with doubts and fears. It's a place where the likes of fishermen and debt collectors find hope and grace. In the light of His revealing love, it's the place where our hearts can finally breathe and experience the quality of life we crave.

Please don't turn away. Don't give in to the feeling of needing to rush your visit. Our hearts have been victimized by the pressures of our world too long. It's time to reclaim the promises that are rightfully ours, to end our fruitless fishing, and to fully discover true fulfillment.

APPARENT VICTIM OF AMNESIA DISCOVERED BY LOCAL RESIDENTS

By CARRIE BULLOCK FISHER

LOCAL AUTHORITIES ARE requesting any information the public may have in the discovery of an adult female whose identity is presently unknown.

Residents reported a disturbance on the south side of town when the victim, wandering along a busy intersection, was approached by neighbors attempting to assist her. Without provocation, the woman in question became agitated when these good Samaritans tried to help.

Police were called to the scene, and the victim was taken to County General for further evaluation.

Hear, you deaf; look, you blind, and see!

GOD (Isaiah 42:18)

Hustling through a small-town grocery, my daughter Georgia and I were shopping to feed a hungry crowd. Several volunteers had gone on ahead, ready to knock out a day's worth of spring chores at a nearby camp for children. We scoured the aisles for ingredients to throw together lunch for our hardworking crew. While I waited for the butcher to slice meat and cheese for sandwiches, Georgia proceeded to gather other items.

It wasn't long before I heard back from her. "Mom, I need the cheese."

"He's still slicing it," I said of the butcher.

Seeming annoyed, she spoke again, "Mom, I need the cheese!"

"Honey, he's not done slicing it yet," I replied.

With perceptible exasperation she tried again: "Mom, I neeeeeeed the cheeeeeeese!"

Georgia wasn't usually so impatient. What was all the fuss about that my twelve-year-old would be so insistent on collecting unsliced cheese? Certain she saw my confusion, I pleaded, "Georgia, what do you want me to do? I can't make him slice it any faster!" There in the middle of that grocery deli, I felt embarrassed that others were hearing such a ridiculous conversation.

Undeterred, she continued, "Mom, I need the keys!"

"Oooooooooh!" I sort of groaned, as my brain finally distinguished a distinct 'k' sound at the beginning of that one word instead of the 'ch' I'd previously understood. Thankful for information that finally made sense, I deduced she needed to get into the car and continued, "The keys . . . of course you can have my keys!"

It would be one thing if she'd been speaking from a distance, but she wasn't. She was right in front of me. Had I known there were volunteers waiting to load bags of groceries into my car, perhaps my ears would've better assimilated the information being presented. Context clues are awfully important, you know? I had cold cuts and cheese on my mind, not grocery bags and keys. Without the proper frame of reference, Georgia's words were reduced to meaningless noise to me, making for an unnecessarily complicated exchange.

In this age of technological supremacy, the sound of noise is all around us. We hear sounds from the other side of the world, from deep space, and from voices of long ago as they're replayed from recorded clips. We subscribe to podcasts, play music from cell phones, and are reminded of the reality of crime and disaster as sirens race past at breakneck speeds. We've almost no choice but to hear. But who are we listening to, and what precisely are we hearing? How do these sounds impact our lives and the lives of those around us? With all this noise vying for our attention, it can be hard to maintain the context of who we are.

We're searching for our true identity, who God created us to be. As we look, we must give ourselves to this process of becoming, instead of settling for who we've become. There's a strong tendency, even for believers, to settle into some combination of our true self and our broken self, a habit we must constantly guard against.

If we're going to function as redeemed and restored individuals and be joined together as one Body in Christ, then we must be mindful that the competing sounds within and around us make us prone to misinterpret God. Our past experiences sometimes leave us tempted to ignore some or all of His words of life to us. These tendencies cause us to flounder in a sea of misdirection, wrong assumptions, and empty living, and we become stuck instead of progressing in our journey of faith.

The restoration of our lives then falters when we react in fear or distrust to freeing gestures meant for our good. Our response tends to be like the gentleman who began merging into my lane on a recent trip into town. I must have been in his blind spot when he began steering his car into my lane. Regardless, fewer inches than I would've preferred were all that separated us from being an unwanted traffic incident.

Startled by what was happening, I honked to let the driver know I was there. Imminent disaster averted, I drove on. As I passed his vehicle, the stranger sped up and sounded off with a prolonged honk of his car horn. Then he slowed to let me pass again as his hand rose above his car window. His one-finger salute left little doubt about his feelings in that moment.

We humans have lots of blind spots, and they often lead to a variety of consequences. My own blind spots began taking root in the midst of a childhood struggle to survive the cravings of an unfulfilled soul. They continued gaining momentum until I was faced with a lifetime's worth.

I had a fear of not being good enough, so I obsessed over my ability to perform well in whatever I was doing. I was determined to earn the respect of others and loathed being corrected. I was afraid I'd wind up unloved, so I held onto my relationships until I drained them of their very life. My reaction to anything that appeared to threaten my fragile existence was one of distrust, leaving me at the mercy of lots of blind spots.

Left in the wake of these misguided efforts and my inability to see beyond my brokenness was my wounded heart. I had difficulty trusting and relating to God; this defect was made worse by the effects of living in a less than perfect world. I wasn't all that different from my highway-saluting adversary. How could I trust and respect a God who seemed content to watch me flounder from such a distance? And like my conversation with Georgia that day at the grocery, how could I relate to a God who made little sense to me in the context of my life as I knew it, let alone trust whether He could make any difference in the quality of my life?

Thankfully, God never stops doing His part. He's a loving Father who persuaded me that He has me on His mind. It took a while, but I eventually realized I'm a child of the Creator. His intentions toward me are trustworthy and carefully thought out. I'm the beneficiary of His goodness. I'm made in His image and bear a portion of His glory, a child whose Father works to bring me to a state of being complete, whole, and sound. I've been invited to enjoy the gift of relationship with Almighty God, and with brothers and sisters made one in Christ.

God is so committed to blessing that not only does He seek to give, He seeks to cause us to receive[1] all that will prosper us in this life. This distinguishing feature of God's character is far different from the notion I harbored for many years. I hadn't imagined that a God I perceived as distant and hard to please was at the very least my loudest Cheerleader, proudest Parent, and most invested and trustworthy Teacher.

When I was a freshman in college, I glimpsed just this kind of commitment. At eighteen years of age, with Thanksgiving approaching, I looked forward to the freedom of sleeping in and having time off from school. As my fellow students headed out for the break, my plans for a relaxing holiday had to be altered. My beloved grandmother, who battled a debilitating illness for most of my life, lost her fight the day before Thanksgiving.

Years before, as a middle schooler, I remember sitting at the table in my grandparents' kitchen. I'd listen for what must've been hours as my grandmother, seated in her wheelchair beside me, filled my imagination with wonderful adventures. Her soothing voice, punctuated by the occasional cackle of her chickens outside, left me mesmerized by lives from a different time. With her stories, she introduced me to her family, and told tales of how they prevailed over unimaginable hardships. These were ancestors I'd never know, except by way of her memory.

Through her eyes, I witnessed people full of life who had a willingness to hope for something more, combined with a steely grit to persevere through difficulties. These were traits that showed themselves to be alive and well in my grandmother, even in the midst of her declining health.

In her presence, all seemed well in my world, so her death was especially hard on me. Just two years before, my dad had unexpectedly passed away. With her passing, it felt as though I'd lost all that was precious and safe in my young life.

I recall returning to my dormitory the Sunday evening after saying a final goodbye to my grandmother and thinking no one had any idea how much I'd lost. The best times of my life were the times I spent at her side. In that realization, I suddenly felt so disconnected from the world.

I hadn't been a real dedicated student my freshman year, but one of my professors was hard to dismiss. His lectures were interesting, and he proposed ideas that got me thinking in ways I hadn't before. With Thanksgiving break over, everyone around me began to gear up for the semester's final exams. I, however, settled into a dejected mindset and this one professor seemed to sense it.

The harder I tried to give up on my academic responsibilities, the more determined he was to see me succeed. Truth be told, I was so far removed from even caring about passing my first semester of college that I considered not showing up to take my exams. Yet this teacher provided extra study sessions and even scheduled a makeup exam for me to allow extra time to complete the class requirements. He simply wouldn't let me fail.

Decades have now passed since that heart wrenching Thanksgiving season. Looking back on it, I was in a vulnerable place, yet the kindness of a college professor to seek me out and hold a door open while taking my hand and helping me walk through, enabled me to hold on. His determination compelled me to stay the course.

I didn't know it then, but his actions toward me were a beautiful example of the dedication the Father has toward each of us, a Father who's invested in us and who'll always make a way to preserve the life He's given us. It's God who didn't give up on me, even as my ears misheard and my eyes didn't see. It's He who continued calling out to me, even as I inched ever closer to the harmful consequences of a sinful nature.

Once I began to grasp the reality of His love for me, not just on the surface, but in the depths of my brokenness, my world began to change. Slowly but steadily, I grasped Whose I was, and in that realization, who I was.

When someone is reported as missing, some of the most helpful tools for locating that person are the most basic; their name, details about their appearance, and other personal information. Yet often our wandering hearts are kept in the dark because we lack a clear picture of who we are, of our destiny, or of this God who loves us so. As we continue our search for the growing life that we have in Christ, we must seek open eyes to see and listening ears to hear from this God whom we can trust, to hear of the blind spots and misperceptions that hinder us from receiving His full work of grace.

The Father's intentions toward us, like my intentions toward a misunderstanding driver, are good. We have an opportunity to hear from our Redeemer and Restorer. If we can find the courage and strength to take Him at His Word and stop resisting His aid, we'll be the beneficiaries of His empowering nature. In our quest for our true identity, we as victims and we as brothers and sisters will discover lives far more alive, connected, and meaningful than anything we've imagined, as our minds and hearts embrace the nourishing Truth of the One and Only.

The Examiner   *May 23, 1999*

AMNESIA VICTIM BELIEVED TO BE LOCAL LONG-LOST CHILD

By CARRIE BULLOCK FISHER

AUTHORITIES BELIEVE THE woman who was rescued from a busy intersection late last night may in fact be a female who went missing thirty years ago as a young child.

Officials have refused repeated requests for information. However, one source, speaking on condition of anonymity, is saying the woman fits an age-enhanced photo, which was taken from the FBI Missing List.

The thief comes only to steal and kill and destroy;
JOHN, THE BELOVED (JOHN 10:10)

"The truth is, sir, you never really play it 100%,
no matter what," said Francois,
the South African rugby team captain.
"Ah," replied President Nelson Mandela,
"in sports as in life." [1]

By the time the disciples found themselves in the presence of Jesus at Mt. Olivet, they knew one another pretty well. They'd experienced glorious highs and agonizing lows together. Over the course of time, some of their individual strengths and weaknesses had made themselves known. They'd learned one another's stories.

Among the twelve, there were brothers, husbands, fathers, newlyweds and bachelors. Some supported aging parents, while others were just coming into their own. A few of the disciples were ostracized by family members for their differences of opinion and viewpoint. There were men who came from well-known families. Others came from nothing. Their educational backgrounds were varied. One of the disciples is considered to have been wealthier than the others.

There were strong personalities, natural leaders, revolutionaries, articulate and loyal followers among them. Some were instantly likeable, while others required some getting used to before the group fully embraced them. Numbered among them were passionate men and mild-mannered men. Some spoke early and often as others guarded their words and chose them carefully. Some of the men embraced attention while others were content to work quietly behind the scenes.

This diverse group brought many talents and strengths into the "Fishers of Men" Mission. And Jesus welcomed them all, allowing each man to grow in his knowledge of Him and to serve as each personality allowed. They were considered to be good men, with the exception of Matthew, whose business practices were assumed to be shady and unfair. But Jesus knew the challenges and setbacks they all faced. He knew even more about these men than they knew of themselves. He knew that each of them also brought into the group misperceptions, blind spots, hurts, and the disappointments that had come their way.

These were men with real weaknesses and limitations. Time and history haven't allowed for an accurate recounting of them all, but we're familiar with some. Peter was impulsive and subject to certain types of fear. James struggled with anger issues and wasn't always honest about his motives. James' brother John also had a temper. He was prideful and intolerant of those he considered to be inferior to himself.

Philip lacked imagination, which hindered his ability to grasp the possibilities of a given situation. Nathaniel tended to judge and struggled with prejudice. Matthew was materialistic and could also be shortsighted at times. Thomas was often too dependent on logic and tended to be overly suspicious. Simon the Zealot was a crusader, without always considering his genuine motivation or the true importance of a cause. Judas tended to hold tightly his own opinions and beliefs and harbored grudges against those who challenged his sense of right.

Surely each of these men's hearts bore the marks of pain and loss. From their limited state, their perceptions about themselves were far different than what Jesus saw in them. Even as He saw the brokenness, Jesus also saw hearts and minds that would be transformed as His love and empowering grace penetrated every facet of their lives. He saw their true identity. As we imagine looking on in the last moments before their Leader ascended to heaven, it's easy to see that the struggles and challenges of these men aren't so different from our own, but it's important we recognize in the midst of our own brokenness, Jesus also sees our true identity.

I was born at a time when parents had children simply because that's what young married couples did. My arrival seems most insignificant considering the United States' population in my birth-year alone would increase by over three-million people[2]. How could I have known I was highly favored by a God, who in His great love had destined me to experience the fullness of life that was already secured for me? Hearts are extraordinary creations of a magnificent God, yet the glory contained within mine never entered my mind.

The depth of relationship I was created to enjoy suffered jarring blows from the start of my existence. I had no idea, nor would I have wanted to hear this, but I was a victim of my limited nature. I was also victimized by parents who tried to raise me well. They weren't bad parents. They were good and hardworking people; but they had their own weaknesses and limitations that would impact my life. Finally, I was victimized by an unseen, yet determined thief who worked quite effectively in my life as the father of lies.

Victimization appears differently in people, especially when the offense isn't recognized. Some who've been victimized live in a state of denial. Others make light or are unaware of their predicament and the effect it has on them. Sometimes victims are filled with self-loathing, believing they deserve whatever suffering comes their way. Or they're overwhelmed or paralyzed by the hurt they've endured. The victimized often struggle with exaggerated fears, feel a loss of control, suffer flashbacks, and endure disrupted relationships.[3]

No matter the response, our human state has rendered us, as it did Jesus' disciples, injured and limited. Our lives are lived on a battlefield. The prize? Our hearts and minds. This is such an ordinary reality that it can be difficult to recognize, yet the consequences play out in any number of physical, emotional, and even spiritual reactions often keeping us in a state of disorienting brokenness.

I'm reminded of a hot, sunny afternoon, sitting in an old pickup truck and looking out onto the sunlit waves of one of my favorite lakes. As a wife and mother of two young children, I was preparing to enjoy a week of family time filled with swimming, water-skiing, and rustic campfire food. I grew up boating and retained good memories of those times, yet as I prepared to back the boat trailer into the water, I began feeling uncomfortable. For no apparent reason, my heart began pounding and my chest suddenly became noticeably tight.

Startled as I was to notice this, I was none the less aware it was a feeling that permeated every boating trip I took. It had never occurred to me, but nestled into those good childhood memories was the fact that going to the lake also made me anxious on some level. With this realization, I quizzed myself: Why was I feeling so tense? Because going to the lake is stressful, I heard myself answer. Why? I pressed. Because I might get yelled at or lose my turn if I make a mistake.

This silent and one-sided dialogue left me surprised. I consider myself a level-headed woman. The thought that such anxiety was buried within my subconscious all those years seemed unbelievable to me. But my physical response left no room to argue. These fears lived. If such an innocent event could trigger this kind of response, what else lurked beneath the surface?

After surviving a lifetime of wandering about with little insight into my true identity, I'd made a deeper connection. Unsettling as it was for me, it was time broaden the search for my identity. I was long overdue to grasp a fuller understanding of who I was. Fortunately, aiding me in this undertaking was a growing sense of Whose I was. In Him, there was safety in looking and discovering. There was purpose in making a deeper connection of all that I was—my mind, body and spirit within the redemptive Hand of God.

My husband, Brian has a habit that our kids and I have resorted to teasing him about. Early in our marriage, I'd sit at the table, wondering if he was enjoying the meal I'd prepared for him. However, Brian doesn't offer his opinions very often, a trait that didn't take me long to pick up on, so I'd invariably ask how the meal was. His answer to my question was most always a reserved "it's good." This short and monotone response left me no way to decipher what "it's good" actually meant. He teased that I expected him to stand on his head to convince me if he liked something I made.

This standoff turned in my favor, however, when he and I were dining at a restaurant for lunch one afternoon. It was a restaurant we visited most every Wednesday for what had become a longstanding lunch date. Over the years, we'd gotten into the habit of sitting with the same server every week. We became so familiar to her that she'd memorized our drink order and our preferences for the meals we ordered.

During one particular date lunch, Brian ordered a meal that was different than his normal fare. After his order arrived and he had time to try it, our friendly server stopped by to see if he was enjoying it. He responded with his usual "It's good," which caused her head to whip around to me as she quizzically asked, "What in the world does that mean?" Watching this scene play out with someone else on the receiving end made my day! It was validation enough that Brian begrudgingly accepted that his version of "good" left a lot to be desired.

It's easy to become lulled into believing our version of a good life is adequate for our time on this earth, so easy, in fact, that we tend to settle into this very state. While growing up, I needed something more than my own good life provided, and the deficiencies I felt made me aware there was a problem. Knowing what to do with the problem was my dilemma. I was a mere child with little understanding in the face of my needs. I didn't know the language of my heart, nor could I find the words to articulate my feelings of insignificance and pain, so I languished there in that familiar place, living the only life I knew while dying for something more.

True goodness is an attribute of God, manifested in us, along with other god-like qualities, as we allow His perfecting love to work itself into the brokenness of our hearts. God-likeness is about change, movement, a spiritual commute that we must actively engage our hearts and minds in. God-likeness produces life. Here on earth, it produces a balance of spiritual, emotional, and physical wholesomeness. The sad truth is, the quality of our lives is often hindered by hearts that have been victimized in a fallen world and by a hungry enemy, leaving us to settle for something less than the Father's goodness.

This is a challenge for all who seek their true identity. We must allow our sense of good to be confronted. We must learn that the best way to honor our parents and predecessors is by pressing on in our pursuit of a restored life, one that's not bound by our enemy's efforts to extinguish that life nor limited by the injuries and fractures that come our way in the course of living. Yet the sounds of rejection, loss, fear and failure don't simply fade into the distance. Childhood, relational and self-inflicted wounds don't heal themselves. The expectations that others have of us, as well as those we hold for ourselves can cripple, frustrate and even exhaust us.

The fact is, this earthly existence gives us all we want in terms of surviving it, yet it also gives us ample opportunity to glimpse how limited and incomplete we are, if we'll let it. As Jesus reminded those in His hearing:

> "It is not the healthy who need a doctor,
> but the sick. I have not come to call the righteous,
> but sinners." (Mark 2:17)

We need this physician! For the duration of our lives, we'll always be men and women in need. If we're going to continue our search for what's been lost, if we're going to become true participants and beneficiaries of the conversation between Jesus and these needy disciples, we must be willing to face our human condition.

We as believers desperately need to give ourselves fully to the quest. We must push through the urge to cover our sin and reach beyond the partial truths that keep us in bondage so our hearts will have a greater working knowledge of the truest benefits of grace. We have a Father who longs to heal us; yet when we insist on forging ahead in the familiarity of our own versions of good and safe, our shortcomings are magnified and our relationships to others suffer.

Reclaiming what's been lost or taken will require the courage of my son, Joe. When Joe was a little boy, he enjoyed swimming in his grandmother's pool. Unfortunately, the wooden deck surrounding the swimming area had deteriorated to the point that aging boards lay in wait to lodge nasty splinters in Joe's little feet.

The task of splinter removal wasn't easy. It was surprising how adept Joe was at thrashing and flailing. He preferred to leave the splinters in his foot than to endure the discomfort of removing them, yet as I watched him, I realized it was his fear of the pain, more than the pain itself, that made him so combative.

Fast forward to this past summer and a now fully-grown Joe. What started as a normal afternoon of boating and swimming at a nearby lake ended in a trip to the Emergency Room. Not a drowning, nor a boat accident . . . after all these years, it was yet another splinter that had gained our attention. While walking on a beach we've visited countless times, Joe stepped on the branch of a Hawthorne tree, known for its abundance of one to five-inch long thorns.

Though we couldn't see for sure, we felt certain a potentially large thorn had broken off in his foot. The ER doctor numbed the area and made a small incision to search for the thorn. I marveled as I watched this boy who'd so feared this process remain calm and still as the doctor worked.

Unable to find anything, the doctor bandaged the wound and sent us to a foot specialist. Sure enough, a second examination, aided by a deeper incision, revealed a two-inch spike lodged deep in Joe's foot. Because of the fear of infection, particularly a bone infection, the foot needed special care. It also had to be monitored for weeks. In the end, his foot healed with no complications.

If Joe had reacted like he had as a child, dealing with the wound would've been difficult. He may have tried to hide the splinter from us, or he may have been so set against going to the doctor that at six-feet, two-hundred and fifty pounds, we would've been powerless to make him go. It was his courage that enabled him to first submit, then endure the discomfort that treating it caused. In displaying that courage, he avoided a potentially serious bone infection that could've cost him a foot or even his leg.

However, Joe didn't just endure the process, he enjoyed it! He relished meeting the doctors and nurses and seeing the concern they displayed for him. He discovered a camaraderie with the other patients he encountered. He felt compassion for a young boy whose injury required stitches, because that little fellow felt afraid, a feeling Joe could relate to. He also took pleasure in the attention from us at home while he convalesced. I think, too, Joe enjoyed the feeling of satisfaction at being courageous in the midst of his fear.

In him, I observed a bravery that would benefit us all. Finding the courage to expose the splinters that have worked their way into the depths of our hearts will take a determined effort, yet restoration awaits; and there is joy and fellowship in this journey of healing.

For many of us, fear is the first assault we must confront as we submit our hearts to God. Truth is confrontational in nature. It digs deep, and reveals much. However, God wishes to expose the splinters, those corrupted files stored within our hearts that stand between us and life. It's the blind spots that leave us vulnerable to hurting ourselves or others that He seeks to bring to the light. It's the fact that by our very nature, we're prone to wandering and hardening, denying and avoiding, all so we can settle into our version of a good life. Our enemy has used every opportunity to his advantage. Time is of the essence because it isn't a foot or a leg, but our very lives, as well as our Body that are at stake!

There's pleasure in discovering the depths of love and compassion in the Father's healing hand, in discovering we're not alone after all, and that His mercy is new every morning. Undergoing this kind of restoration has the added benefit of developing compassion in us, as we relate more honestly to the brokenness of our brothers and sisters.

As the authenticity of our compassion one for another grows, so too will this family of believers as we find ourselves escaping the settlement that has held us too long. We don't have to remain victims whose identity has been stolen or lost. This bears repeating—we truly do not have to remain victims. So much more awaits us.

POSITIVE ID MADE IN YEARS OLD CASE

By CARRIE BULLOCK FISHER

OFFICIALS CONTINUE TO piece together the details of a decades-old missing persons case that has taken such a miraculous turn.

Preliminary evidence confirms the identity of a recent amnesia victim as the child who was abducted some years ago. Evidence also indicates that an unidentified suspect held multiple victims.

It appears the victims had a fair amount of independence, though it seems many did not realize the extent of their freedom.

Sources say the woman came from a well-known family, owners of a large orchard. However, because of her memory issues, doctors are reluctant to speculate on her future.

The cause of amnesia is still unknown, though her impaired state may be due to the years she spent in captivity.

Now the mind of the flesh [which is sense and reason without the Holy Spirit] is death [death that comprises all the miseries arising from sin, both here and hereafter]. But the mind of the Holy Spirit is life and soul peace both now and forever.

PAUL, THE APOSTLE
(ROMANS 8:6, AMPLIFIED BIBLE)

When I was younger, I was befriended by a well-known lady in our community. I was a skinny tomboy enduring the cruelties of junior high. She was a short, round woman living out the last years of what had been a full life. Living right across the street from her, I was drawn to her enthusiastic style. Everything within her influence was abloom with color and vibrancy. Laughter was a common sound in her home.

I learned she was a straight shooter, and she expected others to be as well. At this stage in her life, she hadn't the time nor patience for anything less. This was her time to enjoy these last years with family, friends, and the garden she loved.

Her driveway was often dotted with the cars of her sons, the minister, and many of the friends she'd made through the years. They visited with such regularity that as I arrived home from what would have been another miserable day of school, I knew which car belonged to what person; yet my friend always made time for me. She generally had an after school snack to share, before she and I would load her El Camino and drive out to the country. We'd then spend the afternoon working in her garden. I enjoyed visiting with her as we harvested her bounty of vegetables from the dark, rich earth.

We didn't talk much about it, but I knew she'd known difficulties in her life. Decades earlier, as a wife and mother of two young boys, she'd settled into a comfortable routine. She taught a Sunday School class, enjoyed being part of various social clubs in our sleepy little town, and enjoyed her status as the daughter of a well-known and respected family in the booming 1920s.

Then, as the stock market crashed, her world began to crash as well. Her husband abandoned her and their sons. Shortly thereafter, her mother's health began to fail. Without warning, she found herself with no means to care for her family.

Her desperation grew as efforts to secure employment proved futile. She was fighting the bias of being female, the stigma of being divorced and a shortage of jobs due to what would become known as the Great Depression. I'm certain in light of the obstacles she faced, she cried out for God to provide something, anything; yet my guess is she felt very much alone and lacking in the necessary resources to endure her newly-uncertain future.

After exhausting every opportunity she could find, she stumbled into what would become a profitable business. Her success, however, cost her dearly. My friend established one of the last of its kind, a house of prostitution, in which she as the madam achieved considerable notoriety.

Not surprisingly, she was harshly judged by the religious community during the time her business operated and even after she retired. However, in the years I was acquainted with her, she never expressed regret over her chosen trade.

If I hadn't known her, I might have heard the stories, which by that time were legendary, and seen her the way so many others saw her. But I had the advantage of spending time with her, listening, laughing, talking, and working alongside her. I thought I was being the dutiful, able-bodied young neighbor helping out in her time of need. I'm guessing the more accurate reality is she sensed I needed a friend, a feeling I'm certain she could identify with.

Throughout the years she was quick to give of her time and resources when needs arose. She never abandoned her religious beliefs. Not only did she believe in God, I think she loved Him. She maintained her church affiliation, except, to escape some of negative attention she received, she requested that the minister visit her in the privacy of her home.

In considering the path she chose, it would seem her problems began when her world appeared to be falling apart. She made choices based on what she felt she had to do to survive, yet I respectfully wonder if her troubles only served to expose a faith which was unable to see past her present need.

Her eventual choices seem extreme to our conservative notions. And while it may be easy to second guess her decisions, the truth is, anything we choose, anything we depend on, anything we attempt to work out by means of our own resources, strength, or understanding leaves us in the same predicament my friend was in, living outside the influence of God's life-giving power. And until we can reconcile with that reality, we're in trouble. A world powered by man, where it might seem we're getting by, is a poor substitute for the life-giving resources that come from above. Yet when we find ourselves reacting in a crisis, we're often unaware of what we've forfeited. Then before we know it, we've wandered off course with no idea how we ended up where we are, or how to find our way home.

For my friend, her choices affected her own life in that they brought loss, the loss of experiencing God in the midst of such a desperate place. The lives of her sons were affected by her choices, a sentiment she acknowledged later in her life. Even though she was a good-hearted business owner, surely the influence she had over her employees and patrons suffered loss as well. In the end, only God and she know her true spiritual fate; however, I hope to share more time with my friend in Glory!

Getting beyond the stigma of such a lifestyle and our tendency to judge, the real tragedy is, when we suffer a crisis of faith, we encounter true loss. This isn't just true in my friend's situation; it's true for each of us. This is why Jesus confronted His disciples at Mt. Olivet.

In my own life, the choices I made produced a similar fate. The circumstances weren't as extreme, yet before I reached my twelfth birthday I'd already had a full-blown faith disaster.

I'd always loved the Jesus I grew up hearing about. Not only was church an important part of my upbringing, I already had years of singing gospel music with Dad and my brother under my belt. My first musical performance came at the tender age of four. Mom and I were at home, a little four-room house we were temporarily living in. With no indoor bathroom and just an old pot-bellied stove to keep us warm in the winter, it was an adventure living there until construction was completed on our new farmhouse up the hill.

Dad was a busy man, with increasing responsibility in the road construction business. When he wasn't working, he was gaining a reputation as an excellent vocalist. Along the way, he was part of several gospel quartets before joining forces with a couple of local friends. This newest group became known by many as the best mixed-gender trio in our state.[1]

Dad regularly left for work before we even saw the light of day. Once the rest of us woke up, Mom would get my brother off to school, and I, being the industrious sort, spent those preschool years outside. Between climbing trees, trying to catch fish with no bait and always keeping an eye out for new adventures on our small farm, I was always on the go. But every weekday at noon, I headed inside for lunch, where Mom and I turned our attention to a crackly black and white television broadcast of a gospel music show. It featured recordings of various groups singing many of the songs and hymns I loved. Several of the singers were family friends. And then there was my favorite artist of all, my dad.

One afternoon the show played a recording of Dad singing "How Great Thou Art," a well-loved old hymn. His rich tenor voice captivated me as I listened. After the show was over, I walked straight to our piano, an antique converted player piano Dad had brought home, and to Mom's amazement, my four-year-old hands replayed almost exactly what Dad had sung. After that incident, there was little doubt I'd inherited some of Dad's musical abilities.

I eventually gained Dad's confidence that I was ready for the responsibility of singing with him and my brother, even though I couldn't have been more than six or seven by that time. This was no small commitment. Dad expected my brother and me to have each of our songs memorized and polished to perfection. We spent hours each week practicing song after song including working out creative harmonies so our performances were more than the curiosity of such young children entertaining on an adult stage.

In many ways, our lives revolved around Dad's passion for music. I can remember more than once being awakened at night because company had dropped by. Mom would get us up so we could join Dad to sing a few songs for our guests. We performed in churches and what was referred to as 'singings,' travelling all around most every weekend.

I can remember singing before our state governor, a man who somehow managed to hold the respect of his constituents throughout his term in office. Even though I was young, I felt honored to be in the presence of such a well-respected man. I still have preserved audio clips where, after we'd finish singing, preachers and church leaders alike would say what a blessed family ours was, and how special it was that such precious children would be devoted to doing good.

It was around the time my brother's voice began changing that the dynamics of our family trio began changing as well. I've never spoken with my brother about it, but I'm certain there was more going on than his growing larynx. Our schedule had become routine. Dad worked long hours during the week and on many Saturdays. In the evenings when he came home, I'm guessing my brother began to tire of the demands Dad made of our practice time.

Even more, I wonder if he wanted something more from his time spent with Dad than singing. Regardless, my perception was, when my brother began to balk ever so slightly at the practice time and intensity Dad insisted on, it was over. Dad made up his mind, and sadly, we'd never sing together again. I don't think Dad realized an alternative solution could've been found.

In many ways, I think this is when we lost Dad. He stopped singing for the most part and began working even more. He came home even later in the night; so late in fact, I was usually in bed, occasionally hearing the sound of his vehicle pull up to the house as I drifted off to sleep. On Sundays, if he stayed home, he slept, probably to make up for working such long hours. Work for Dad began consuming so much of his time, he became too busy to go church, the very place that had hosted us on many a Sunday when we were singing together. Even when he bought an old ski boat, then later a houseboat, my brother and I often had to pass the time quietly so as not to disturb him from resting.

In recalling this period, I see some red flags that were imperceptible to me then, things that would've complicated my spiritual and emotional growth. The way my world revolved around Dad; that I learned to value performing at a high yet superficial level; the fact that I felt abandoned by Dad in so many ways, even though I realize that wasn't the intention of his heart. Also disturbing is that I was so drawn to a religious culture yet for whatever reason, I failed to grasp a deeper understanding of the message.

The first signs of my religious troubles came during a church revival, of all things. I was eleven years old. Nearing the end of that service, our pastor gave what was known as an altar call. I'd sat through many of them. This call was an invitation for listeners to reflect on the spiritual state of their life and to come to the altar for prayer if they chose.

Everyone prepared to sing the hymn for this invitation. As if on cue, the hands of young and old alike reached for the nearest book of hymns, causing a distinct scraping sound as the hymnals rubbed against the rack. As people stood, some of the smallest children, who'd been sleeping on their parents' laps, resettled into the pew, heads lightly bumping the wood as they resituated themselves. Sounds of Bibles closing and knees popping here and there were sprinkled in for good measure. After a verse or two, the piano continued to play softly as the pastor spoke a few more words.

For many of us younger participants, the serious nature of this time eluded us. This was evident in the whispers and occasional bursts of hushed laughter from the last couple of pews in back of the church. Over the years, I'd come to look forward to this portion of the service. Usually it meant one last song, and then we'd head for home. But on this night, the unexpected happened. I sensed something; a feeling of discomfort, undoneness. Riding home with Mom and my brother, I felt troubled, unsettled, and uninterested in the conversation going on between them.

This was a church Mom had moved us to after Dad no longer accompanied us, and I'd settled into a cozy existence there, until the night of that holy nudge. The feeling awakened something within me that reminded me of my spiritual emptiness. After the service and throughout the next day, my mind attempted to process what my heart was trying to tell me, a task I didn't have much experience with.

As time for the next evening's revival service approached, I became uneasy. Then after an hour of hearing about the horrors of an eternity spent in hell, my discomfort must've been evident because Mom leaned over to check on me. She asked if I'd like to pray with the preacher at the altar. Why I'd be so reluctant, I don't know, but her gesture enabled me to summon the courage I needed to ask for prayer.

In that particular church, it wasn't uncommon for others to join in praying at the altar. During this collective petitioning, some kneeled silently while others prayed aloud. It was an experience; one in which I have fond memories. Except for this one time, since I was now the object of their prayer.

I mumbled something to the minister; I guess enough to communicate why I was standing there. He asked me to kneel for prayer. The intimidating task of walking down the long aisle, to speak with the preacher in front of all those people behind me now, I began feeling better, excited even, because this was, after all, something I'd always wanted.

As I closed my eyes, I prayed the words I'd been taught for years. I knew I was lost and needed the saving work of Jesus. I knew I was a sinner because that's what I'd been taught. I asked for forgiveness from my sins. As I prayed, the voices from others around me pierced the air with pleas on my behalf, many of them continuing to grow louder. I said what I knew to say, but everyone else kept praying. In time, their voices began trailing off, until all was quiet.

The preacher asked if I felt better. The thing was, I didn't feel any different. A bit embarrassed, I answered, "No sir." In all my years of church services, I don't think I'd ever seen the prayer not work! Maybe I was the first, to be honest. Sometimes at the conclusion of a sinner's prayer, the individual now saved by grace would be so happy he or she would begin to shout or weep. Other times she or he would talk quietly with the pastor. But the outcome was always the same, a new believer was welcomed into God's kingdom. Yet, there I was, beginning to feel a bit nauseous while admitting I felt nothing.

So the preacher had us all pray again. This time, my prayer wasn't motivated by the specifics of my eternal need. I was fighting for my dignity in what felt like a more immediate need. God, please save me (from this demoralizing situation)! I'll do anything (so I can tell them I feel better). Please, Lord, I need You (to help me save my reputation)! I was pleading with a newfound sense of misdirected urgency, accompanied by the prayers of intercessors who were completely unaware of my panicked state. As neighboring voices began dying down, I stood and summoned the will to survive the humiliating question that awaited: "Do you feel better now?"

The innocence of a child died that day, as waves of confusion and conflicting emotions settled into my consciousness. I felt no peace as I lied and mumbled "Yes sir, I do." I couldn't wait to escape this new sensation of shame I felt. It didn't occur to me that one doesn't easily outrun such torment.

The long shadow cast by that experience stretched into every corner of my life. By day I kept the emptiness at bay by staying busy, but by night, when the darkness in the air seemed to call out the darkness and shame that lurked in the depths of my soul, I suffered through waves of panic complete with heart palpitations, nausea, and night sweats. Haunting my consciousness was the feeling I had genuinely sought Jesus. And it seemed He didn't show.

I never thought for an instant His absence was because there was no God. I believed in Him down to my very core. Therefore the only other possible explanation was that somehow this child, for whatever reason, was unworthy of His attention.

I carried my shame like a prisoner secured by a ball and chain. Not understanding the true spiritual heritage I had access to, I didn't realize I had a choice. I dared not speak to anyone about it; after all, I'd been given two chances at getting it right. How could I let others know how unfit I must be?

My shame complicated my already crowded survival agenda. The emotional deficit that had been growing within was now compounded by all of these newfound emotions from the spiritual disaster I'd now endured, and I remained a hostage to it all, like my friend the retired madam and so many others I've met through the years. All I knew was that I had to find a way to survive my shame and captivity.

The Examiner　　　　　*January 19, 1969*

FUTURE OF RESCUED WOMAN UP IN AIR

By CARRIE BULLOCK FISHER

AUTHORITIES ARE SAYING A woman rescued after spending decades in captivity is dealing with her new-found freedom as well as can be expected. She remains in treatment.

One source close to the case states her prognosis is good, though he said victims often have conflicting feelings about their time as a captive while adjusting to their new life.

She is the daughter of a wealthy orchard owner, but there is speculation she may not return to her home.

Regardless, her Father has committed to pay for all expenses toward a full and complete recovery.

I am the LORD, the God who cares for and sustains
His people; in Me, you and your children
will receive a good heritage.
Over the course of time, you'll see obstacles
and encounter difficulties, but in Me,
you will succeed.
Your faith will provide others a glimpse of Me,
and they'll be the better for it.
Truth will take root in their lives. It will affect
future generations, bringing hope to the weary
and salvation to those who've lost their way.
I am with you wherever you go;
I'm here, and I keep My promises!
-CARRIE BULLOCK FISHER
(PARAPHRASE OF GENESIS 28:13-15)

When I was a child, I talked like a child,
I thought like a child, I reasoned like a child.
When I became a man, I put the ways
of childhood behind me.
PAUL, THE APOSTLE (1 CORINTHIANS 13:11)

When Joe was in fourth grade, Brian's parents took him and Georgia to explore some of the West Coast. While travelling, Joe and Georgia experienced many firsts. They flew over the Grand Canyon. They swam outdoors in a desert swimming pool in the dead of winter. They saw the Mormon Tabernacle Choir. They explored Death Valley. They paid a visit to the Golden Gate Bridge. And these were just some of the highlights!

Throughout their travels, it was Joe's perspective on the trip that provided the most entertainment to Brian and me. During one phone call home, Joe proclaimed his hotel room was exactly like our house. When I asked him to elaborate, he said it had beds, a bathroom and a TV just like we did at home! Since we lived in a large two-hundred-year-old house that likely had little in common with a small hotel room, his dad and I snickered in amusement.

On another call, I asked Joe to describe the best thing he'd done on his trip. Without hesitation, he blurted, "Oh, that's easy! Watch TV!" His perspectives were often unexpected and entertaining.

Centuries ago, I wonder if the disciples didn't see a similar tendency in Peter's growing faith. One minute he'd perceive the impossible and the next he'd default to his best guess.

When Jesus was arrested prior to being crucified, Peter anxiously positioned himself close by, beside a warming fire. Some servants also gathered nearby to see what the commotion was about, along with some Roman soldiers, who waited outside while the proceedings against Jesus wore on.

Peter wanted to be close enough to keep an eye on this hasty arraignment, but he was nervous, so he tried to hide in the safety of the shadows. This was after he proclaimed his loyalty to Jesus, the Man he dearly loved. Yet in spite of this fact, he was on the verge of his life's most shameful act. Jesus had warned him about his tendency to react, but Peter was sure those days were behind him; confident his devotion to God would sustain him through anything.

As the dawn of a new day hovered over Jerusalem, a rooster awakened. Though it was still dark, one of the servants saw Peter and wondered aloud if he wasn't one of Jesus' followers. Panicked, Peter dismissed the servant's words. Shortly thereafter, a maid caught sight of him and said she was sure she'd seen him with Jesus. Again, Peter contradicted her, swearing she was wrong. By the time another group of bystanders realized Peter's identity, he began cursing them all.

Across the yard that rooster stood tall, then began to gently flap his wings, just enough to fill his lungs with air. Then that rooster proceeded to proclaim to all within hearing distance that this was his territory with his "Coocckkk-a-doodle-dooooo." There was no missing it, nowhere to hide. Peter had done the very thing he was sure he could never do. And in the last remnants of darkness, Peter glimpsed the depth of his brokenness.

I was a mere twelve years old, yet spiritual fulfillment seemed out of my reach. That's an overwhelming thought for a burgeoning adolescent whose heart longed to be known and cherished. Full of determination, I forged ahead in life, lugging my secret baggage of disappointment and shame all the way. I had no inkling of what God's perspective might be.

I saw one option; keep myself together, keep moving. Things had to get better.

A few years later, one dreary spring morning, I was mostly sleeping through a tenth-grade Driver's Ed class. Hearing my name over the loudspeaker caused me to snap back to consciousness. I had no idea why I'd been summoned to see the principal. Making the tedious trip from my classroom near the gymnasium, I turned down the dark hallway leading to the school office. I don't remember who directed me to the principal's door, but somehow, as if by magic, it opened and I walked in.

At sixteen years of age, losing a parent had never entered my mind, yet here were familiar voices saying things like "your dad" and "a construction accident." Amidst these shattering words my heart began to pound. My mind raced as I felt myself begin to shake ever so slightly. My mouth, suddenly quite dry, found swallowing and speaking difficult; yet I pressed on. "Is he okay?"

And then a pause, one of the longest pauses I've ever known . . . I don't recall if it was Mom or the friend who was the attending State Police Officer at the scene of the accident. I remember my ears straining to focus while everything else in me seemed to go numb, sensing the outcome, yet praying I was wrong. "No, he didn't make it."

The next few days were a blur of people. After that initial adrenalin burst, shock and numbness overtook me almost completely. A friend of Dad's arrived at the house and worked his way through the large number of visitors who'd taken up vigil with us, making a point to seek me out. Opening his arms wide, he drew me into him and said, "Let it all out." But there was nothing; I had no tears. I was unable to articulate any emotion. A bit embarrassed by my lack of a response, all I knew was, I just felt so empty.

Life afterwards within my family became an everyone-for-him/herself kind of existence. No one intended it to be that way, but it was. In many ways, our lives had been defined by Dad. I was having a difficult time imagining my life without his. Feeling alone, I wandered on through the rest of my high school years.

By the time I limped into adulthood, I was fatherless. The close-knit family I longed for seemed forever out of my reach. Feeling disconnected, I continued to harbor tremendous shame and agony over the questionable state of my spirituality, as the God of my childhood appeared to be equally distant in my adult life. I should've been poised to make my way in this world, yet without understanding why, I'd lost my way without even realizing it.

One consequence to feeling so lost was how much my past influenced everything about my present, including who I married and why I had children. It defined all my relationships, including my superficial relationship to God. It influenced how I reacted to adversity and where I turned for answers, if I actually sought answers. I became a driven woman, but I was driven by all the wrong things.

In spite of this, I managed to get by. I modeled what was familiar to me. I was hard-working and good-natured. I was a committed servant of God. While only vaguely aware of my true motivation, my unfulfilled soul pressed on in pursuit of acceptance, respect and attention.

It was important that I involve myself in the right activities. I had to present myself and my young family in the right way. Go to the right church, know the right people. These tendencies never struck me as potentially wrong or harmful. I was simply trying to provide the influence and security that would help me overcome those lingering feelings of powerlessness and insignificance.

I remained a victim, even to the perspectives I banked my happiness on. Like Joe, I saw things a certain way; therefore, I reacted and interpreted everything in life according to this limited way of seeing, yet my perspectives weren't cute and entertaining like Joe's. Mine were more like Peter's, killers that were sucking the life out of me, out of my relationships and out of my faith.

It was a full twenty-three years of anguish before I gained peace about my spiritual condition. As the soccer coach of Joe's young team, I also helped out with the rest of the soccer program at Joe and Georgia's school. Since we were in the midst of a rainy spring season, the kids' Saturday morning games were at risk of being cancelled.

This particular morning was shaping up to be no exception, and it was up to me to make the call. In the midst of the downpour outside, I set off for the soccer fields to assess their condition. I then rushed toward home to cancel the games before anyone else ventured out into the wet mess.

I didn't account for a sharp curve about halfway home. As wet as the roads were, there was no chance at making the turn at the speed I was travelling. In all the years I've been driving, I'd never had more than a couple of minor fender benders before this slick curve. That all changed when I hit the brakes to try and slow down. As I lost control of the vehicle, my van slid off the road and went airborne on its way to a wooded embankment several feet down and away from the road.

I felt no panic while deducing my chances at survival depended heavily on how and where I landed. Loose change and various bits of debris, some rattling and some flying, came toward the front seat as the nose of my van plummeted. In that instant, time seemed to stand still, and for the first time in my life I was at peace, full of faith; perhaps like Peter when he proclaimed Jesus to be God's living Son during one of his moments of brilliance. In faith, I realized if I didn't survive this landing, I'd be heaven-bound. It was a gift; forget surviving my most harrowing car accident ever.

When my vehicle came to a sudden stop several feet from the road, I realized I'd suffered no injury. After a quick phone call home to ask for help, Brian and his dad arrived on the scene to examine the vehicle. Amazingly, my van wasn't damaged. All it needed was a tow back up to the road. From there, I was able to drive home. The real miracle that day wasn't my unscathed body or van; it was that after all these years, I finally rested in my heavenly Father's acceptance!

Despite this knowledge, my life didn't experience any great change. Like Peter hiding out in that darkened courtyard, and like the rest of Jesus' disciples before that day on Mt. Olivet, I continued living, reacting, and interpreting mostly as I always had. My faith remained as vulnerable as the disciples' as they struggled to grasp and hold onto the life-changing truths they were discovering in their time with Jesus. I eventually ended up exhausted from trying and failing to survive life on my own.

A few years later, I found myself in need of having an MRI scan. I was dealing with some back pain, and after two rounds of physical therapy and some unhelpful x-rays, the doctor suggested the MRI to get a better view of what might be the source of my problem. He asked if I'd ever had an MRI and I told him no. He said I'd do fine, and they weren't that bad. If he thought those words would put me at ease, he thought wrong because I immediately began worrying about why he'd say such a thing.

After some research, I discovered that MRI scans, which at that time were performed in a closed tunnel, are a walk in the park, as long as you like parks contained inside a small body-sized tunnel, and you don't mind being strapped inside a tight space while being told not to move while having mere inches between your face and the hard, cold structure of that tunnel. Unfortunately, I have a pretty good case of claustrophobia, so this sounded like no walk in the park I'd willingly submit to.

By the morning of my appointment, I was quite anxious. I didn't know how I was going to submit to such a procedure, given the confining nature of it.

Before I headed into town, I spent some time reading my Bible. It was my latest, but also my most desperate effort to cultivate a more intimate spiritual connection. Chronically uninterested in Bible study, I'd begun asking God to give me a love of His Word. I was reading through the Old Testament and the passage that morning ended in Genesis, chapter 28 where I read these words:

> . . . Surely the Lord is in this place and I did not
> know it. (Verse 16, Amplified Bible)

It was a story about a dream Jacob had with a ladder that led to heaven where he encountered God. I had a hard time relating as I read through the chapter, but I was serious about developing this discipline, so I finished my reading. After getting ready and making the short drive into town, I nervously took a seat in the imaging waiting area.

While I waited, the words I'd read earlier began to sink in and take on new significance:

> Surely the Lord is in this place and I didn't know!
> This place here . . . with me!

Within minutes, the radiographer escorted me to the scan room.

Armed with this revelation, my outlook on that tunnel changed dramatically. It was a narrow tunnel, and I was still claustrophobic, but I wasn't alone! In one glorious moment, my mind, imagination, and heart grasped that I'd had a divine appointment with God that morning, where He assured me He'd be present with me during a routine MRI scan. Instead of panicking, I found myself, even in the confines of that narrow tunnel, rejoicing in God's Presence, a feeling I'd never known.

Then I began to realize it wasn't just the tunnel! He'd been there at that church altar all those years ago. He'd been with me every time my heart felt abandoned, every time I cried out. He was present as I struggled to accept the loss of my dad, and when I lost my grandmother. Through every moment of my life, He was there; I just hadn't known it.

For a world full of reasons, I hadn't been able to incorporate all those spiritual truths I'd grown up hearing about. I hadn't been able to imagine and internalize them enough to make a deeper connection in my heart, until that moment. This newfound knowledge infused my spirit with courage, hope, and, more than anything, a love that felt so personal. His presence, and my ability to perceive His presence, began to change everything in me. It enabled me to finally enter the work of transformation, of becoming my rightful self.

Unlike most followers of Christ I've known, I honestly can't say when Jesus heard my prayers and gave me the gift of salvation, but I know when I discovered I was His. I found Him while I was wrecked. I found Him again in the broken places of my life. After a lifetime of wandering, there was no more standing on the outside looking in; I was beginning to find myself, restored in Him.

PART II

THE LEAST OF THESE

MAN ON FIRE

By CARRIE BULLOCK FISHER

A HORRIBLE SCENE UNFOLDED earlier today when a young man became engulfed in flames. The cause of the fire is unknown at this time.

What is known is that the victim was seen running down the street, apparently attempting to outrun the fire. Witnesses reported that many onlookers failed to offer help while others fled the scene. Upon further questioning, several individuals claimed they didn't notice the man. Some also stated their fear of becoming injured themselves.

For now, doctors say the victim has extensive injuries and is clinging to life.

I saw the darkness when no one else saw
And felt the weight of an unknown flaw
Alone I questioned, alone I groped,
Yet the answers weren't what I'd hoped.
Then the darkness set about its quest
Of taking a child from his mother's breast
To a state of madness, a dreary place
Leaving only the slightest trace

Of the boy I'd known so well and loved so much,
A boy who might've been president
Or a preacher or such.

Eventually others began to see,
And accusations flew at me.
Surely I'd done something horribly wrong,
But the darkness only soldiered on.
Defying explanation and resisting aid,
Manic swings left me afraid.
How far to the edge? How long can he last?
How much can we take in a house made of glass?

From the boy I'd known so well and love so much,
A boy who might've been president
Or a preacher or such.

Fatigue and sorrow weigh down this weak frame,
Yet I press on, and with conviction proclaim:
All is not lost, the darkness will end.
My child will prevail, his spirit will mend.

As I yearn for the boy He knows so well
And loves so much,
The boy He could've made president

Or a preacher or such.
More than anything, I know the boy lives
In the palm of His hand
Where darkness will give way at His command.
-CARRIE BULLOCK FISHER

I was young when I glimpsed the potential destructiveness of fire. Dad had come home from work early, an unusual occurrence. Normally the shortened daylight hours ran out long before his truck pulled into our driveway. As he entered our house, I noticed his uncertain gait.

He was talking to Mom. While my brother listened in to their conversation, I focused on what he was doing. My normally sure-footed father sat on the bed to balance himself; then he gingerly lifted his pant leg, revealing a bandage which completely covered his lower leg. Even with the bandage on, I could see a large wound beneath that spanned the circumference of his leg. It looked quite gruesome.

Earlier in the day, Dad had stopped by a job site where some of the crew had started a fire inside a metal bucket. It wasn't uncommon for construction workers to do this, using less volatile diesel fuel to clean the stubborn asphalt off their shovels and rakes. They'd also toss in whatever trash happened to be lying around. During the chill of those winter months, the fire-bucket also provided a way for the crew to warm themselves out on the job.

While Dad was inspecting their work, he accidentally kicked the fire-bucket, setting his pant leg ablaze. The fire burned through to his sock and leg underneath. Thankfully, because of the cold, he was wearing gloves. Dropping to the ground, he began rolling and patting out the fire with his glove-covered hands. His burns were serious enough to send him to the doctor, but his quick thinking prevented further damage.

On another occasion, my young mind was again troubled by damaging fire. It was a chilly Thanksgiving afternoon. From the warmth of my grandparents' kitchen I watched as my dad, grandfather, and uncle worked outside. They were trying to crank an engine in an old car that had languished in a field beside the barn for as long as I could remember. My uncle had decided to restore the car, and it seemed the perfect activity to work off the extra calories they'd eaten a few hours earlier. While they were working, a fire erupted from under the hood. In horror, I realized my uncle's upper body was enveloped in flames.

The way he took off running is a sight I've never forgotten. The flames intensified in his brief strides before Dad caught up to him, tackling him onto the ground to suffocate the fire. He suffered severe burns that required treatment and some time to heal.

Both of these incidents made an impression on me as I cringed at the ugliness of those painful wounds, yet I never imagined there were fires that rage unseen, and that injuries from these internal infernos could be equally painful.

Joe was my firstborn, the child whose delivery brought the longed-for gift of motherhood to me; the child I assumed was the answer to a prayer I'd prayed for much of my life. To all who asked during my pregnancy, "What are you hoping for, a boy or girl?" though I hoped to have a boy first, followed by a girl sometime later, I chose to voice what I thought was the most appropriate sentiment: "I don't care as long as it's healthy."

Perfection is what I saw as my eyes first beheld this life that had come from the hidden safety of my womb. This wasn't just any two-eyed, ten-fingered, ten-toed newborn. He was mine, and he was the recipient of a mother's heart that was full of love and hope for a fulfilling life.

Those first few years of parenthood were typical of most new parents'. Brian and I settled into a life of less sleep, dirty diapers, and all kinds of wonderful new memories. Of course, our hearts grew to cherish this growing child of ours with each passing day. Within a few months, our perfect son became a bit sickly, suffering chronic ear infections and full-blown asthma attacks. Even though we became more familiar with hospitals and emergency rooms than we ever imagined, we took this in stride, even gaining the friendship of Joe's pediatrician along the way.

Aside from the complications of his asthma, Joe was an easy baby. The occasional dinner at a fancy restaurant proved painless as baby Joe napped while Brian and I enjoyed a nice meal. In the midst of major house renovations, Joe contentedly slept or played for long stretches while the family dog watched over him.

If I wanted to entertain a friend for lunch, I learned to have a cold watermelon on hand so I could send Joe out to our fenced-in play area with a slice. As I watched through the windows, he'd find a place to sit on the jungle gym his dad built and work at that piece of watermelon until he'd eaten every speck of pink. Then, with watermelon juice pasted all over his face, running down his arms, and dripping off his hands, he'd come knock at the back door. I'd give him another piece and off he'd go again. It was a sure-fire way to keep him occupied.

It became apparent early on that this little blond-headed, blue-eyed boy liked people, a lot! When Joe was five, we signed him up to play t-ball. It wasn't that he expressed an interest in playing; I just assumed that's what all five-year old boys were supposed to do, learn to play competitive sports.

We were new to the community and didn't know anyone at the ballpark, yet the excitement of Little League baseball hung in the air. After Joe's turn at the tee during one of his first ballgames, he sort of jumped/hopped his way to first base as I cheered from the bleachers. Another teammate batted, and Joe's coach yelled for Joe to run to second. He was doing so well; surely he was a natural!

It was while Joe was waiting on second base that things became interesting. Coaches of the opposing team were allowed to be on the field to direct their novice youngsters. So the other coach happened to be standing close to Joe. Joe took it upon himself to make a formal introduction. It was so cute! As the next young batter was having some difficulty hitting the ball, Joe's conversation with the on-field coach continued. Finally, the batter got a hit and went running after first base.

As we parents cheered for this particular batter, we noticed a rather lost-looking boy who'd moved off of first base. With a new runner headed to first, he should've been running from first to second. I'd become distracted by this latest hit and wasn't paying attention to Joe. Surveying the playing field for a reason as to why the runner from first to second base looked so out of sorts, I narrowed in on the problem. Instead of running to third base, my Joe was still in deep conversation with the opponent's coach!

Unaware of their expectation for him to run to third and being oblivious to the bewildered boy who needed to be where he was, Joe kept talking. His coaches began yelling for him to run. We parents yelled for him to run. Joe's teammates were yelling for him to run, yet while the other boy stood looking so forlorn, Joe continued visiting away. Who even knows what he was talking about? What does a five-year-old go on about with a man he's never met?

From the bleachers, I could tell the opposing coach finally suggested Joe might ought to make his way to third base. At his recommendation, Joe took off like a little man on a mission. With his baseball hat cocked ever so slightly to the side, fists clenched and arms flailing, Joe began running as fast as his legs could carry him. It was the most entertaining moment of t-ball I ever witnessed. It was also Joe's only season to play on diamond-shaped fields. If that exchange was a precursor to his disinterest in the sport, it was also a window into his enjoyment of people.

In spite of Joe's outgoing nature, there were signs of trouble. A year later, at the Christian school we enrolled him in, a mother of one of his classmates asked me to call her when I could. Having gotten to know the children in Joe's class, I'd also become familiar with many of the parents. I was caught off guard by this mom's request, however, since we didn't normally exchange phone calls. I assumed she had a question about an assignment or some sort of school business.

When I phoned her later, I was dumbfounded when I learned the purpose of her call. She explained there'd been a situation at school involving her daughter and my son. Her daughter had become upset because someone told her that my Joe wanted to have sex with her.

I burst into nervous laughter; not out of disrespect, but because I thought a punch line must be coming. Surely this was some sort of joke. Yet as she kept talking, it began to dawn on me that she was serious. My demeanor went from disbelief to mortified shock as I apologized profusely for her six-year old hearing such a thing and promised to deal with the situation.

My mind was racing. What in the world could have happened? As I contemplated our conversation, I began to have questions about the plausibility of the incident. I wasn't trying to dismiss what this mother said, but the story didn't add up. We'd been careful as parents to know what kind of influences Joe had access to. For the life of me, I couldn't make the leap of what I believed his level of knowledge regarding this adult topic was to what he'd been accused of.

Not only had we shielded our kids from such talk, neither of them were the daring sort. They liked to know and obey the rules, especially at school.

Working to collect my thoughts, I called Joe outside for what had shaped up to be a beautiful spring afternoon. Away from Georgia, I motioned for him to join me on the porch swing, where the birds, unaware of my agitated state, sang away in the trees above. Working to suppress all of my shock, I began quizzing Joe about the girl in question. Since his dad and I hadn't begun teaching the kids anything about the finer points of boy/girl relationships, just figuring out how to broach the subject of "having sex with her" was a bit flustering.

At a loss for a clever way to back into the conversation, I braced myself and, as gently as I could, I went for it. "Joe, did you say you wanted to have sex with Lindsey?"

By the perplexed look on his face, I knew he was clueless. He looked up at me with those innocent blue eyes and quizzically asked, "Zex . . . what's zex?" His response made it clear he was a long way from insulting any girl about such things.

Curious as to what had actually transpired, I called a couple of moms from the class, moms I knew and trusted. To my surprise, after these moms spoke with their sons, they confirmed that all the boys in the class knew of the rumor, but had no other information.

It occurred to me to call one more mother. Though I wasn't as familiar with her, her son was a likely candidate to provide more insight into this mystery. He was a cute little fellow, with curly red hair. A big talker, he was the kind of guy who worked hard at looking cool, yet who'd wilt as soon as heat came his way. I had a hunch, if there was something more to the incident, he'd talk.

For all us protective mothers, this was scandalous stuff. Therefore I was confident his mother would be determined in her efforts to get to the bottom of the matter. After a short while, the mom called back with the inside scoop, which confirmed my suspicions. The boy explained that another boy in Joe's class master-minded the whole story. This instigator, well-liked but a bit of a bully, made the whole thing up, even going so far as being the one to inform the girl of his make-believe accusation. Of course, the girl was horrified, and told her mother.

Since it was apparent this prank had become the talk of the class, I informed the teacher of what happened. She made all the boys appear before the principal. Joe was sent as well, not because he was in trouble, but because he, too, had been victimized by the prank. Poor Joe; always wanting to please. He couldn't shake the feeling that he was being disciplined. Joe's conduct at school was so important to him. When teachers let him work on assignments out in the hall, he would tell everyone who happened to walk by, "I'm not in trouble. My teacher's just letting me work out here." Having to appear before the principal was something he'd never experienced. The whole episode left him wounded and embarrassed.

This was my first major clue that, despite Joe's outgoing nature, he was not faring well with peer relationships. There were other signs as well. Family get-togethers provided opportunities to observe Joe's unsuccessful attempts to fit into social gatherings. Though he was trying, he didn't seem to possess the social wherewithal to interact with even his cousins the way he wanted to. It was a point that couldn't be missed; this boy who loved people of all ages and types wasn't succeeding at being social.

There were other indicators that something was wrong, behaviors and deficiencies that seemed innocent enough by themselves, yet in considering the overall picture, I had a growing sense that something wasn't right with him.

By the time Joe was entering adolescence, when he should've been making strides toward becoming more independent, he continued a pattern of falling further behind in his ability to accomplish the simplest of things. He was chronically disorganized. His ability to master tasks ranging from personal hygiene to preparing to run an errand to following simple instructions was deficient. Yet everyone around me felt this was boyish behavior that would be replaced with the experience and maturation that would inevitably come.

But it never did. Joe began to have constant meltdowns at home, and his need of so much oversight was beginning to take a toll on me. What had seemed somewhat manageable in his earlier years began taking most of my energy and resources to get him through any given day. I was no professional, but it was clear that these problems were more complicated and extreme than a simple case of immaturity.

School was becoming a disaster. Joe was behind, unprepared, disorganized, and generally lost regarding his academic responsibilities. There was mounting pressure from many of his teachers since they believed he was capable of more. After all, he was a good boy. He was outgoing and eager to please.

Surely he could do better, they challenged. He needed more discipline, or better organizational aids; or he needed to be pushed harder. Surely I was teaching him to be this helpless, one teacher accused.

I was exhausted from attempting to help Joe succeed, that's for sure. I'd tried talking and reasoning with him. I'd purchased all the organizational tools I could find. I offered motivational ploys. I attempted standing back and allowing him to fail. I allowed him to experience natural consequences . . . you name it, I'm pretty sure I experimented with it, yet nothing worked, leaving me with the conclusion that my Joe needed help.

So I tried to guide him through the most important assignments and responsibilities so he wouldn't seem so unprepared. Who cared about passing grades? The real prize became appeasing Joe's teachers to try and minimize their frustrations with him. Thank God, Georgia was a self-reliant student.

Through the many years Joe spent in various public and private classrooms, he had a few incredibly patient teachers along the way. Unfortunately, Joe often found himself on the receiving end of many of his teachers' frustrations since his academic performance was so poor. The teachers who remained encouraging and respectful always made his and our life so much more tolerable.

Joe's adolescent years grew more troubled. My dream-come-true child, once so easy-going, had somehow grown into an explosive nightmare. It seemed he was being overtaken by a growing and menacing stranger. Sometimes when Brian or I attempted to merely lay our hand on him, he'd react as if we'd pushed him, then he'd throw himself across the room. It was an alarming reaction.

During a long drive on one vacation, he turned the back seat of our van into a military shrine, pasting war-related pictures all over the back of the vehicle. His defiant demeanor underscored the troubling seriousness of his mindset.

At age twelve, during a trip away with his grandparents, Joe met up with an older adolescent who introduced him to the concept of Internet pornography. It was a vice that became quite powerful in Joe's life since he was so unsuccessful in developing healthy relationships. Discovering his newfound form of entertainment, Brian and I punished him. We also began monitoring his computer time, yet hyper-vigilance didn't erase the images from his lonely mind.

Joe had always been artistic, so in his continued pursuit of soothing his isolated heart, he took to sketching obscene images and leaving trails of hand-drawn sleeze everywhere he went. His preoccupation exceeded that of adolescent boys. Joe had begun exhibiting obsessive behavior about many things. This x-rated fetish soon became one of the more worrisome.

It wasn't long before Georgia stumbled onto his stockpiled collection of hand-drawn vulgarities. To that time, we'd somehow succeeded in keeping her out of the worst of our nightmare with Joe. She was about ten when I began having the first of what has become many conversations with her about Joe's issues, even if we didn't have a name for them at the time.

Of course, the kids battled with one another nonstop. Neither found much to like in the other. Georgia was so young and Joe's behavior was all she knew, so to her, the fighting seemed a normal part of life. Even as they fought, she assumed this disturbed environment, along with his constant agitation was normal.

This wasn't what I wanted for either of my children. I feared I was losing Joe even as Georgia's innocence was being shattered. I explained to Georgia that Joe wasn't well, and that we were looking for answers and trying to get help for him.

As things continued to escalate, she had no choice but to grow up quickly after that. She'd been our baby, but as Joe's illness evolved and the depth of his need unfolded, the birth order began to take an unnatural and dramatic shift.

Somehow, in only a few years, my life had evolved from the wonder of motherhood to the reality that we were facing sobering challenges. Joe's behavior didn't stand out enough for anyone other than me to realize something was gravely wrong. The extreme degree of his inability to function was hard to fathom unless one lived with him. The range of his negative emotions was growing more extreme, yet confined mostly within our presence. Despite seeking help from doctors and mental health professionals, it took a load of laundry to prove the precarious state Joe was now living in.

In the thirteen years I'd been washing Joe's clothes, I learned the hard way it was best to go through his pockets first. He'd long ago adopted the habit of using his pockets as a handy trash and storage area. Along the way I also learned how to best remove ink from entire loads of whites and gum from fabric. I air-dried billfolds, preserved school correspondence, and salvaged completed but misplaced homework.

I found missing ID's, bus passes, and loose change. I always welcomed the discovery of whole dollar bills. I grew especially thankful that his dad was knowledgeable about electronics for all the gaming and musical devices in need of disassembly so they could air-dry. Brian's success rate at salvaging water-logged electronics was worthy of admiration.

One morning I busied myself with the now standard practice of emptying and sorting through the crevices of Joe's pants pockets. As I smoothed out wadded and wrinkled papers, my eyes fell on a disturbing sight. There, on a single piece of paper, was all the evidence necessary to prove my concerns and get the help Joe needed.

Things were worse than I'd imagined or understood; the state of Joe's mind a reality no mother wants to discover. There, on tattered paper, was proof that Joe was in trouble, irrefutable evidence that the days of innocent "zex" were long gone. Joe's pornographic drawings had taken on a dramatically violent and threatening tone.

This was a young man who was growing overwhelmed by urges and longings he had no healthy outlet for. Forced to live in a world that either bullied or dismissed him, he was a lonely and tormented soul. His longing for acceptance and relationship was fast becoming a breeding ground for a growing rage toward those he held responsible.

This was not my son! This was a delusional stranger whose thoughts were reprehensible. Filled with shame and grief, I wondered what had gone so wrong.

This evidence was undeniable. So the psychiatrist rededicated himself to Joe's treatment. He compiled a profile based on mine and Brian's family history, Joe's behavior and his life experiences. I was hoping there would be some kind of pill for Joe to take that would make it all go away. Instead, the psychiatrist explained that Joe had a complicated and difficult to treat form of schizophrenia.

I'd lost Dad prematurely. I lost my grandmother, too. Over time, other losses came; but this one has proved to be the most painful. Getting this diagnosis felt like an ending. I feared the worst, that my child had become an uncontrollable monster.

There was good reason for my fears. This agitated stranger living among us with his irrational outbursts and rages, combined with the sheer size of the man he was becoming, gave me plenty to worry about. While Brian often travelled because of his work, I remained at home with Joe. The smallest thing could set off an outburst so extreme that on more than one occasion I feared for my own safety. I'd lost my son and inherited an overwhelming burden.

He was almost impossible to live with in so many ways. But concealed beneath a misleading exterior was a boy in immense pain. He was like a man on fire and running for his life; running to stop the pain, yet instead, he found the intensity of the flames increasing with each desperate step. Instead of me being able to help, to stamp out the fire, it seemed he was dragging me right along with him.

Eventually I came to see Joe was still in there. What seemed a burden became a calling. We found mental health professionals better equipped to help us care for Joe. A host of strong medications helped stabilize the chemical imbalance occurring within his brain, easing the worst of the psychotic thoughts he was having. But as that first psychiatrist warned, the bulk of Joe's symptoms remained at the mercy of behavioral therapies and coping strategies that have been difficult for his impaired mind to implement.

PROMINENT FAMILY THREATENED BY FIERY FALLOUT

By CARRIE BULLOCK FISHER

A RECENT FIRE-RELATED disaster has a local family in the hot seat, authorities say. The family, long known for their success in the fruit production business, has a growing scandal on its hands. Trouble emerged when a fire broke out, severely injuring a young man.

Family members failed to satisfactorily answer investigators' questions about why the victim received no treatment immediately after the fire. Reportedly, the family is claiming the man in question was of no relation to them, though his identity has been confirmed.

While no one has been charged, the fallout has been damaging. This isn't the first time police have visited the family compound. A child was kidnapped from the family over two decades ago.

The child was eventually rescued, but she has remained estranged from most family members.

"The family has been disintegrating for years," one family friend said, "yet no one wanted to believe it could come to this." Now it seems another life hangs in the balance, while a family is left to ponder these lingering questions.

" . . . whatever you did for one of the least of these,
. . .you did for Me."
JESUS OF NAZARETH (MATTHEW 25:40)

Father, I want those You have given Me
to be with Me where I am, and to see My glory,
the glory You have given Me . . .
JESUS OF NAZARETH (JOHN 17:24)

When Georgia was a little girl, she knew what she wanted. Her single-minded purpose in life was the pursuit of mine and Brian's undivided attention. I can still recall her precocious tone as she demanded, "Hey, watch me!" and "Look at me!" over every little thing she did. She insisted we take notice of all her accomplishments, and not as passive onlookers, but as eager observers, marveling over each of her great feats.

It proved to be a helpful trait. Joe didn't demand this kind of attention, but his disability necessitated it. As his illness evolved, it could've been easy for Georgia to feel overlooked as Brian and I reacted to the roaring fire of insanity, yet her boldness cultivated within us a keener awareness of our need to tune into our golden-haired girl beyond what our increasingly compromised intentions might have provided.

It turns out Georgia isn't the first person to seek attention. Throughout His time on this earth, Jesus taught, and even more, provoked His disciples to focus on Him. "Behold," He said on numerous occasions. It was another way of saying, look at Me! Jesus was instructing and appointing this flawed group of men, preparing them to lead the way into a bold and impossible calling: becoming the Body of Christ. With each word, He challenged His disciples: look at Me!

I can almost hear Him saying it, a sense of urgency piercing the airwaves, leaving little doubt of the importance these words held for His followers, along with His desire that, in hearing them, the disciples would respond with that same sense of urgency.

Just to submit their hearts and minds to Jesus took a leap of God-given faith. This was the Son of God they'd joined with, after all! In their wildest dreams, had they ever imagined such a possibility? Even so, I'm certain it remained an ever-present challenge to keep looking beyond themselves, beyond what felt right to their stubborn senses, beyond their comfort zone. Jesus was constantly pressing them to look with the eyes of a Spirit-driven faith at truths they were incapable of perceiving on their own; at a glory they desperately needed to glimpse.

The circumstances the disciples faced in practicing this new way of seeing weren't what I'd consider ideal, yet the disbelief, confusion, and persecution all around them were precisely the conditions Jesus chose to remind them: look at Me! He urged them to see a reality that surpassed what their physical senses discerned, beyond what their circumstances dictated.

Scripture records numerous accounts illustrating the difficulty they had in keeping their eyes fixed in His direction, especially when He appeared in unfamiliar ways as He did on Mt. Olivet that day.

For the disciples, leading up to that glorious Ascension Day, pesky rumors had begun to circulate. Like those boasters insisting they'd seen a risen Lord. Why hadn't the disciples seen Him if He was truly risen? They were the ones Jesus was most loyal too, they reasoned. And anyway, they'd seen Jesus perform miracles, it was true, but that was when He was alive. He was dead now. It made no sense why people would claim He'd actually risen from the dead.

And so, seeing with their eyes and reasoning with their minds, these disciples were stuck. Until the Man they could recognize appeared before them; the Man who'd once again challenge them to seek the truth with hearts of faith.

I can imagine my own reaction if I'd been in the disciples' shoes. I would've wanted to believe, wanted to see, yet I would've had parameters. Knowing me, I'd have been fine looking at Jesus as long as He was behaving Himself, showing up in ways I could tolerate. I could trust I was seeing Him in the lives of people I respected or had things in common with; at the very least, people I considered as equals. But I also know me well enough to know I'd tend to be dismissive of anything that didn't conform to my expectations. Regrettably, encounters of the divine through individuals I considered inferior to me were likely to be dismissed.

My time for looking for Jesus wasn't with the disciples on that day, and presently my sight has been jarred by a painful loss. Somewhere along the way a dream was shattered, a dream precious to this mother's heart regarding the son I envisioned raising, the son I worked so hard to give the life I imagined for him. Yet I can hear Jesus as He continues to say, "Behold" . . . look at Me! as urgently as I imagine He said to His disciples.

It feels a bit risky, sharing much about Joe's struggles. I'm mindful of the stigma and erroneous assumptions often made by many who encounter Joe and others like him, yet I've discovered there's more here than meets the natural eye.

Out of Joe's burdened life has come great revelation. You see, Joe's illness exposes far more about us than him, those of us who walk with him on a daily basis as well as those who encounter him from a distance. His life has given me an opportunity to glimpse how disconnected the Body of Christ is.

Before my very eyes, Joe has become someone Jesus would've referred to as the "least of these." Hungry, thirsty, a stranger, naked, sick, and imprisoned; in so many ways, Joe has become all of these; hungry for a quality of life and for relationships that elude him; thirsty for the peace of a still and sound mind and the respect of others. He's become a stranger in our world, as his confused and irrational thoughts strip away the covering of culturally acceptable normalcy.

A friend of mine knows a similar burden. We met when our sons began the tenth grade at a small school that catered to special-need students. Since that time, our sons have gone in different directions, yet she and I have maintained our friendship. One afternoon while sitting in her kitchen having lunch, I noticed a photograph on her refrigerator. It was a childhood picture of her son prior to the time his problems with mental illness emerged. Wide hazel eyes, friendly with a hint of good-natured mischievousness about them, an inviting smile, and a handsome and carefree face were preserved for the ages.

I commented on how sweet a picture it was, and my friend smiled a conflicted smile and said she kept it there to remind her of how he was before.

Oh, how I can relate to that sentiment. It's not that I stopped valuing Joe's life once he became so challenged. It's just that it's so painful to watch him struggle, especially knowing that his earthly existence may never get easier. And honestly, something I've realized about myself in the midst of this adversity is that I'm stronger than I wish I had to be. Truth be told, I tend to want life to be easier, neater; and with more instant gratification than Joe's illness allows. His condition has changed so much in all our lives. There's genuine grief over what feels like so much loss, yet there's much to embrace about our circumstances.

While my own pictures and memories of easier times remain precious, I believe there's a spiritual journey that awaits all who are willing to enter Christ's presence with people like Joe, even as it exposes our own brokenness, for it brings us to the One who willingly redeems and restores, and who gives dignity and honor.

God doesn't shy away from our troubled hearts if we can find the courage and humility to look at Him and see His presence, even when He reveals things about us through people like Joe. There's purpose in Joe's life in this valley. He has a costly yet precious task; offering the benefit of a looking glass to a broken and disjointed Body.

In looking at Jesus, His disciples must've been reminded of all they were not. In seeing Him, they saw themselves more accurately. It had to be humbling, yet also freeing and empowering. All these centuries later, if we know Christ, then Joe gives us opportunity to see Christ, appearing out of character and in ways that feel unfamiliar and even uncomfortable to us.

If we'll just look deeply enough to see, we have an opportunity to experience something amazing. But seeing with such depth is challenging. When one encounters someone living as the "least of these," more times than not, one sees many things:

- a busy life (their own) leaving no room for unplanned or seemingly unnecessary interruptions,
- the wasted life of someone who hasn't tried hard enough to become successful,
- the failures of others,
- an opportunity to 'help' someone in need in any number of ways, or
- needs of a stranger that simply overwhelm.

Under the veil of darkness a long time ago, poor Peter was having trouble seeing. With all his moments of brilliance, there were such monumental disasters. Jesus kept warning the disciples about the limitations of their flesh, yet their attention, including Peter's, continued to wander. So after that Last Supper together, after hearing Jesus' last sermon, having gathered in the Garden of Gethsemane, Peter unwittingly found himself in the middle of a hostage-taking crisis.

And he reacted as any honorable man would. He fought for Jesus' safety. Producing a wide-tipped machete, he severed one of the ears of the high priest's servant, yet Peter's defense of Jesus was met with a holy reprimand. Jesus told him in essence, "Peter! Be done with your good intentions and those fears that drive you. Stop trying to fix everything with your limited understanding. And for Pete(r)'s sake, stop reacting to your circumstances!"

What Peter was having difficulty seeing in the face of that servant was his own need of saving. He saw chaos and confusion. He saw his comfortable world being threatened. He saw a Man he loved in danger, but he didn't see the greater miracle unfolding right before his eyes, nor did he understand how desperately he needed to see so he could be saved from his own unproductive way of living.

Peter's proximity to Jesus and the glory about to be revealed offered the hope of grace, the hope of becoming empowered to live free, to know the love of God even as the process of grace was carried out within him. But he had to look in faith. Even as those temple guards threatened to wipe out Jesus' very existence, Peter needed to see beyond the surface. Just reading about it, this centuries old dilemma, it's easy to feel for Peter.

This kind of seeing is hard for us, because we must be looking to see, and hard because we must be willing to see. And one other thing, we must be humble enough to see, which, in all honesty, is often our greatest challenge. But the benefit of seeing? It holds the same promise for us as it did for Peter. One of the miracles I'm reminded of most every day is that in Joe, Jesus still calls out, Behold . . . look at Me!

Of course, we're not always aware of the Joes who touch our lives. We're not always aware of how our choice of action or inaction betrays what lies within our own hearts. When we do dare to look, like Peter, we often try to fix what we perceive as being the problem instead of seeing the true solution.

What would it look like to have an authentic encounter with Jesus, to see beyond our comfort zones and the predictability of our lives? Consider the prophet Isaiah's response, when he encountered God:

Woe is me! for I am undone . . . (Isaiah 6:5a KJ)

For him, that divine glimpse revealed the brokenness within his own heart.

Our greatest opportunity, yet also our most difficult challenge, is to become seekers of God. Drawing closer to

Him will reveal our brokenness. But this is our hallelujah, for in this place His glory is revealed in us.

Like us, the disciples had so many opportunities to see; like the time after Jesus miraculously fed the five-thousand. Actually, it was more than five-thousand since wives and children accompanied the men who were counted, but I digress. Picture this; five measly loaves of barley bread and two small fish. Andrew, the chief administrator for logistical operations, had to scrounge to come up with this small pittance of food, yet Jesus had no trouble in taking their resources and multiplying them to satisfy the need.

It was later, as the disciples were boating across the lake unaccompanied by Jesus, that trouble arose. The Sea of Galilee, which is more of a lake, has some similarities to Lake Erie. Though different in size, both are relatively shallow at 200 feet at their deepest point.[1] The waters from these shallow lakes are far more vulnerable to being whipped up by the energy of windy conditions.

I've glimpsed the power of crashing waves from the shores of an Ohio shoreline looking northward onto Lake Erie during foul weather. Modern-day boats engineered to perform and withstand those very waters look small and vulnerable when that ferocious wind kicks up. I can only imagine the concern that arose when the wind set in on the disciples that particular evening. Seasoned fishermen they were, they knew those shallow waters were capable of swallowing their small vessel along with each of them in a heartbeat.

These men were firmly in the ranks of discipleship. They were fresh on the heels of this gaudy miracle of five biscuits and a couple of sardines which accomplished what I have trouble doing with a well-stocked pantry and a strapping six-foot-four-inch son, satisfying the hungering. Yet, in the midst of their familiar world, they fell right back into survival mode, as we tend to do today, as we try to keep our heads above water.

They saw something in the distance. Exactly what, they weren't sure. It was a presence that made them feel uncomfortable; terrified, actually. And then Jesus called out to comfort them, "It's Me!" Continuing on, He said, "Stop being afraid!"[2]

Do you know that a chronic paralyzer and distorter of truth is fear? I see this in myself and in others when the storms and unfamiliarities of life bear down.

Back to that intense scene, who else but Peter would choose to get a closer look at Jesus? Even if it meant he had to defy gravity to do it. Realizing he was powerless to cross the water on his own, he asked Jesus to tell him to come. I like Peter's thinking. If Jesus told him to come, then Jesus would have to empower him to do it.

Out of twelve men, why only Peter? No one else was moved by Peter's boldness? I wonder if the rest of them didn't care to be, or feared being exposed as inadequate, like Andrew possibly felt with his fish sandwiches just hours before. What kinds of things lurked below the surface of their motivations in that instance?

What lurks behind ours? That's what encountering Jesus does to us. It exposes. Peter's boldness didn't shield him from exposure. He stepped into the water the same man he'd been, but as he began to sink from the weight of his unbelief, he did what we must keep remembering to do; he asked for the grace or empowering to do this impossible thing Jesus called him to do.

My life wouldn't be what it is without the experiences I've shared with Joe. Our stories are connected through the twists and turns of his life and illness. It was Joe who had the final say in allowing me to shine a light on his struggles.

What gives him the courage to permit me to do this? I think he has a bit of Peter in him, a faith that's willing to risk him being exposed. He knows his story is filled with brokenness and failures, yet he trusts who and what he sees enough to risk. He knows he's a part of the Body of Christ and recognizes what I've seen as well: there's a growing crisis in this divinely-joined family. Thankfully, Jesus continues to coax and prod through Joe and others, still saying, look at Me!

PART III

A WINDOW TO THE SOUL

The Examiner   *November 1, 2006*

QUALITY CONTROL ISSUES THREATEN VITAL FRUIT CROP

By CARRIE BULLOCK FISHER

SCIENTISTS ARE SCRAMBLING to determine the cause of a growing and far-reaching fruit shortage. The fruit in question is grown by a family who is also being questioned in a separate criminal investigation.

A decline in overall harvests, coupled with a higher than normal incidence of diseased fruit, has gained the attention of botanists who say there is reasonable cause for alarm.

Experts say the family was caught off guard by the shortage and has been reluctant to reassess its farming processes. Now the concern is, will fruit production meet the demand during the upcoming season?

Stay tuned for updates on this story, as our ongoing investigation continues.

Therefore, my dear ones, as you have always obeyed [my suggestions], so now, not only [with the enthusiasm you would show] in my presence, but much more because I am absent, work out (cultivate, carry out to the goal, and fully complete) your own salvation with reverence and awe and trembling (self-distrust with serious caution, tenderness of conscience, watchfulness against temptation, timidly shrinking from whatever might offend God and discredit the name of Christ). [Not in your own strength] for it is God Who is all the while effectually at work in you [energizing and creating in you the power and desire], both to will and to work for His good pleasure and satisfaction and delight.

PAUL, THE APOSTLE
(PHILIPPIANS 2:12-13, AMPLIFIED BIBLE)

A Blind Man Will Not Thank You
for a Looking Glass[1]

It was the middle of summer, hot enough that the grass I was mowing seemed to plaster itself onto my sweat-soaked skin with every pass of the lawnmower. I was sticky and itchy, feeling as if the contacts in my eyes must surely be bulging with dirt as a hot breeze brought clouds of dry dust blowing onto my face. I noticed my neighbor approaching, so I made my way to meet him, cutting the engine to the lawnmower to better hear.

"Would you please not blow the grass from your yard into my garden?" he sniped. I must tell you, his request touched a nerve. I felt blood begin to pulse in my sweaty head and sensed the hair on the back of my neck rising.

Taking a deep breath so my nerves could settle, I managed a sincere apology for my lack of attention and assured him I'd pay better attention in the future.

This is an example of the struggle I have in looking at my sin. My natural inclination is to defend or deny my shortcomings and weaknesses at all costs. It isn't a habit I consciously adopted, yet as I look back I can easily identify the effort I've put into evading the true reality of my life, that I am, in fact, incomplete and unfinished.

Followers of Christ are reminded to walk in the Spirit. I'm beginning to realize it matters how we walk. At fifty-plus years of age and with achy joints making their presence known now more than ever, I've begun paying more attention to the physical mechanics of walking. With a back and neck that scream at the least irritation and knees that crackle and pop like cereal, it's painfully clear my gait has been compromised by some poor habits. Those habits have resulted in a less than desirable effect on my joints and muscles.

Our spiritual walk is similar. As sure as the fruit of the Spirit lives, the effects of the tug-of-war with our fallen nature exists as well. Because of this, our reactions are often influenced by feelings of scorn, suspicion, prejudice, alienation, intolerance, antipathy, and selfishness; all characteristics which stand in contrast to the godly fruit that comes from the pure-hearted.

When someone like Joe comes into our world, someone whose presence threatens our perceived walking path including our plans, our comfort level, or even our faith, our hearts are often exposed as not completely pure. This isn't a good feeling, a fact I was reminded of in the presence of my neighbor that hot summer day.

I don't believe Joe's struggle is the cause that needs to be articulated. It's more that his life is a reminder of the call to each of us, if we'll allow ourselves to hear it, to embrace the process of working out our salvation. It can be tempting to work out so many other things. It's what I spent decades doing in my own life, and it's where the disciples repeatedly veered off course.

Joe's lack of social skills and hygiene are put-offs to most. Behavioral inconsistencies make it easy to dismiss him as a misfit without giving him a second thought. I've seen it in the countless times he's been left waiting because Christian "friends" say they'll do something with him only to stand him up; and in the image of him left alone as, again, more Christians exclude him from their camaraderie. These images have played out far too many times. Sadly, it's easier for some to ignore Joe than to consider the deeper issues lurking within their own hearts.

Sometimes, armed with good intentions, people try to fix Joe, or they try to advise him or rush his growth. In the absence of satisfactory results, they often become disinterested and even frustrated by him. Each time this happens, Joe must deal with the shame of not measuring up. On more than one occasion, he's lamented, "Do they think I want to be this way?" Of course "they" don't realize his illness has left him little choice.

As Joe's mom and advocate, I've been the beneficiary of similar reactions. The few times I've felt desperate enough to request help, I've been reminded, "the Lord will provide." I believe He will, but the dispassionate way these words are often spoken is disheartening. Another attitude I frequently detect, usually from Christians, is that if they had charge over Joe, he wouldn't struggle with mental illness.

These experiences underscore how real the disconnecting forces that exist within this divinely empowered Body have become. They reveal a troubling theme: we're often reluctant to draw nearer to the looking glasses in our lives, especially if those looking glasses pose the threat of exposing issues we'd rather not acknowledge.

And then there's the matter of that troublesome fruit, the result produced by the manner in which we're walking. How can we so easily overlook those within our own Body? Perhaps the better question to ponder is how have we lost so much? When did we become so overwhelmed, walking in a way that's left us out of touch and disconnected? Why have we become so protective of our version of life, even as the joints and muscles of our Body cry out?

I know that the Body of Christ isn't well. I see it in the way we see, or don't see, Joe and others like him. I feel it in the lifestyles we've become hostages to. This world seems to throw its version of life at us so fast, just holding on can be a workout; yet if we don't actively engage in the walking out of that ongoing process that is our true life, we're further compromised in our ability to live and love out of a spirit-infused faith.

Years ago, my father shared a principle he chose to live by, which was, do only what you're good at. I sure did love my dad, but even at thirteen years of age, this struck me as flawed reasoning.

His mother had adopted a similar approach, a story we grandkids had heard and laughed about. She'd ordered both of her young sons to stay out of the water until they learned to swim. Well, it was obvious to us grandkids, you can't learn to swim if you don't get into the water!

It seemed to my teenaged mind the same premise held true with Dad's thinking. There was no wiggle room for growth with such a philosophy. I saw the consequences of this play out in how Dad chose to invest his time and resources, in the expectations he had of his family, and ultimately, in how he lost his life.

As new parents just settling into our first home in a new state, Brian and I began attending a small church where a particularly endearing man was the minister. Pastor Bob, as everyone called him, had a good-natured sense of humor which served him well, especially at home, where he was the lone male among his wife and three young daughters.

Pastor Bob didn't have a lot in common with the members of our little church. He wasn't from that area. Many in the congregation were decades older. Several were farmers, with a few businessmen and women among the number. Pastor Bob enjoyed books and history; he spent a great deal of time contemplating life and spiritual matters. However, his determination to, not just love, but to serve each of us there was obvious.

Mixed in among memories of meals shared together and his reassuring presence during hospital stays is an impression that stands as most endearing of all. Brian and I had undertaken a fence building project. Using rough-sawn oak boards we located at a local mill, we were excited about our design and the safety it would provide from the busy road in front of our house.

A church friend had loaned his tractor, a trailer, and a fence post setter which drastically reduced the amount of time and labor the project was going to require. We also borrowed a concrete mixer, but we were still looking at a big job.

Several nights, one almost broken finger for Brian, and a Saturday of prep work took care of setting all the posts in the ground, as well as installing the framework for the fence. Though still enthusiastic, we were feeling the effects of our hard work.

By the time Sunday came around, Pastor Bob got wind of the big project underway at our house. On Monday, Brian who was thankful to have a desk job to escape from all our labor, headed to work. As I busied myself with the morning's chores, I heard an unexpected knock at the front door. It was Pastor Bob, offering to work on the fence.

I was surprised; not just because he'd shown up out of the blue. Pastor Bob was many things, but a handyman he was not! But he felt he could hammer nails into boards, and he wanted to help. As cooler temperatures gave way to the sun overhead, Pastor Bob allowed me to serve him lunch.

After a brief rest, he returned to his work, growing more tired as the day wore on. Blisters began forming on his hands, but he worked on. At the end of the day, an exhausted Pastor Bob gathered his things, said goodbye, and headed home. Truth be told, he didn't get that many boards installed. But what he did accomplish was far more valuable.

Pastor Bob's hard work renewed our resolve for finishing the task. Beyond that, we felt genuinely cared for. His labor of love that day took him far from his comfort zone. He risked being exposed as an inadequate carpenter so he could be available to love.

As followers of Christ, we've been called to embrace our weaknesses and to be thankful for our shortcomings rather than attempting to hide or avoid our areas of weakness. Not so we can have a built-in excuse for our failures, but so we're available for God to work through us and within us.

Accepting a healthy view that, in our present state, we're incomplete and unperfected frees us from harmful tendencies. Because when we don't, our hearts are left wide open to things like pride, fear, and shame. As upside-down as it seems, the humble embrace of our imperfections has the added benefit of enabling us to love others more purely and effectively, like my friend Pastor Bob.

Without a dedication to this degree of honesty with God, ourselves, and one another, we end up like Adam and Eve. They're the ones responsible for the first cover-up debacle— one that ended up setting a strong precedent for generations to come. Overwhelmed with shame by their failure, their efforts at concealing their sin led to a radical new idea called clothing. Yet the rustic apron they hastily devised failed to soothe their undone state.

So they didn't stop there. They continued seeking ways to cover over their shame by blaming anything and everything they could think of instead of looking in faith at what was happening within their own hearts. In short, they were reduced to reacting out of their newly held agendas to maintain what became a flawed perception of what was good in their lives, like me with my neighbor that hot summer day.

It can happen so subtly. Or it can have such deep roots within our existence that we're unaware of our own cover-up attempts and agendas, yet the consequences of these influences affect the motives and judgments of good and well-meaning Christian people as we encounter those around us, including the weak and lowly. In this flawed holding pattern of our avoidance, we often fall into the deceptive guise of putting forth our best effort in Jesus' name, yet our actions betray our pesky agendas.

It's in witnessing others responses to Joe that I've begun to realize our efforts at anything, with the exception of knowing God, come at our own and likely someone else's expense. That's a broad distinction, but one that must be considered. All too often, the secretive agendas that haunt us impart consequences we've not fully understood.

So what are some of the issues at work beneath the coverings we've fashioned for ourselves? The insecurities have been glaring for me. I wanted my children to become well-adjusted and successful adults, hoping their success would further prove my worth. Then there's my lack of patience; my temper when things don't turn out the way I want them to; jealousy that can unexpectedly creep in; my need to provide a perfect life for my kids. There are reasons for that, arising out of that wounded place in me that longs to spare them of the pain and disappointment I experienced. Did I mention pride? Oh yeah, it's in there as well. So many agendas, so little time!

In working out our salvation, we've been invited to embark upon a process, yet for a culture that's accustomed to so much in the way of 'pre-processed' convenience, it can be difficult to know how to submit to such a process.

For instance, Jesus once said He was the Bread of Life, which I think means He's the Prize of the Process. Those within Jesus' hearing knew far more about the process of bread making and of its importance to their survival than we generally do. In a world where processed food has become a major industry, we're used to running to the grocery to pick up a loaf of bread, which is usually made with inferior ingredients and laced with preservatives to ensure a longer shelf-life. We then add that bread together with an abundance of other foods that were unheard of in Biblical times, so that the bread itself is more of an afterthought.

Those within the sound of Jesus' voice knew firsthand that to eat of a loaf of life-sustaining bread, grain must be grown, harvested, thrashed, and milled just to make the flour. From there, the flour would be mixed with water, salt, and a wild yeast, then hand-kneaded until the presence of the developing gluten was strong enough to provide structure and texture for the loaf.

They knew how dependent the entire process was on them doing their part in the baking of the loaf. But they were also aware of how dependent they were on God to provide the conditions necessary for them to accomplish each of the tasks required. The resulting bread was nutritionally superior to what we can easily obtain, and its presence on the table was a ready reminder of the value of the process, as well as the partnership they shared with the Almighty.

We, on the other hand, are left with a growing awareness that the preservative-rich bread we have such easy access to may not be so good for our health. That's a far cry from the imagery invoked by the Messiah all those years ago. Bombarded by the pressures of living in and conforming to this instantaneous, pre-processed mentality that's become so pervasive, it's tempting to acquiesce to that pressure. We've studied and heard and know of God's transforming love, yet we often find ourselves reacting to the pressure of our present realities.

Believers don't set out to deprive the hungry and thirsty, or abandon the lonely, or leave the naked exposed. We just don't always see them, and we haven't realized the far-reaching destruction of our own flawed behavior.

Because of our tendency to short-change the process, our well-intentioned faith has reduced us to the role of workers trying to carry out the burden of Christian life as best we can. However, the fact remains that a mind can't grasp what the heart doesn't fully know, so our words ring hollow and our gestures, those we dare to make from our protective shells, fall pitifully short. Consequently, our fruit is suspect.

This is where I found myself all those years before; full of good intentions, yet naïve regarding God's amazing grace and His transforming power. I remained lost to the effects of my undoneness, even as life beckoned. Just as Christ spoke the truth to His disciples time after time, He's willing to lovingly expose our blind spots and uncover the broken places we've worked so hard to conceal.

The reflex instinct within us would have us turn away, but this causes us to miss out on the invitation to draw ever closer to the glory that God has placed within us. It's all so counterintuitive to our senses. We're put off by shame, or pride; or we're busy, or it feels too overwhelming. Followers of Christ have been invited to participate in the process of working out our salvation. This is the most important work we can ever do.

But it's not just our thoughts and agendas that lead us astray. Just as Adam and Eve fell victim to the lies of the enemy in the Garden of Eden, this same foe lurks in our midst. His greatest feat is for people to think he doesn't exist or that he's having little influence over our behavior or character. As we give ourselves to the reality of our brokenness we must also acknowledge that we are at war with a determined adversary. Now more than ever, we need divine empowering if we're going to receive all God has for us.

With our eyes set firmly on our Redeemer and Restorer, the work of salvation can transform in ways we haven't fathomed. Because it isn't just the Joe's of the world who are hungry and thirsty. The exposed, unhealthy, and imprisoned aren't merely lost souls on the streets, in hospitals, or in shackles. And strangers aren't simply someone else's problem. The "least of these" is also you and me, for we're desperate for Christ to be formed within us, for the Bread that will satisfy the depth of our spiritual hunger, to quench our thirst to be accepted for who we are—royal heirs and limited subjects all mixed together in a humanly maddening fashion.

It is we who are desperate to have our vulnerabilities divinely covered over and protected; to be healed of our brokenness; to be freed from all that would make us less than what God has made us to be; to transform the quality of our fruit. It is we who make up the Body who need the life-sustaining breath of God constantly breathing that life into us.

If we can summon the courage and patience to join the process of working out our salvation where we are weakest—in the areas where we are least, if we'll risk being seen and even known in the places where we're not always handy or good, then we'll find ourselves in Him. And by our fruit, the world will recognize us as God's own.

The Examiner *January 18, 2007*

TROUBLED FAMILY FAILS TO SEEK HELP

By CARRIE BULLOCK FISHER

IN THE MIDST OF A LENGTHY investigation, authorities have determined the actions of a well-known family to be suspect in more than one open case.

After conducting extensive searches and interviews with family members, sources are privately saying they discovered several instances of hazardous materials, security lapses, and questionable oversight within the family complex.

One of the focal points in their investigation is the question of why the family did not call for help in several instances, including that of a young man who was seriously burned last month. Officials have declined to give further details regarding this inquiry since the investigation is ongoing.

The family, a major supplier of fruit, has fallen on hard times since taking over management from the family patriarch.

Maintaining their innocence of any wrongdoing, several family members are organizing a protest and have pledged to fight these findings all the way. However, legal experts are saying any attempts by the family to dispute the charges will only compound the family's problems.

. . . God sets Himself against the proud
and haughty, but gives grace [continually] to the
lowly (those who are humble enough to receive it).
JAMES, SERVANT OF GOD
(JAMES 4:6 AMPLIFIED BIBLE)

Another summer's brutal temperatures had begun their surrender to the inevitability of a cooler fall. And just like that, Georgia was preparing for her sophomore year of college and another year of on-campus housing. Her dad and I volunteered to help with the move. As Brian grabbed several pre-packed boxes, he began urging Georgia to get a move on. It seemed moving had become his theme for the day, yet his pleas went unheeded as Georgia proceeded at her own unhurried pace. Brian was becoming frustrated at Georgia's apparent lack of movement, despite the absence of a mutually agreed-to departure time.

True to his nature, Brian began the day with visions of executing an efficient move. His plan was to get everything packed, loaded, transported to the new place, and unloaded. If this could be accomplished in record time, then so much the better. However, for Georgia, there was more going on than this physical move. A thinker and planner by nature, she was preoccupied with the possibilities of this new school year.

She wondered about the personality of her new roommate and whether they'd get along. She thought about her teachers and the classes she was scheduled to take. She also wanted to enjoy her last bit of time at home with us before the demands of school caught up to her. She planned to finish packing her things for moving; she just hadn't gotten to that part of the plan yet.

To Brian, whatever these distractions were, they were preventing Georgia from doing what he reasoned to be the day's all-important task. His differing priorities fast losing ground to his daughter's chosen strategy, Brian's irritation continued to rise; a standoff seemed eminent. It wasn't easy for Brian to relinquish the supervisory role he'd naturally gravitated to, but since this move was Georgia's responsibility and not his, it was a role he needed to relinquish.

Whether he'd choose to tolerate her differing priorities, and even more, yield his agenda to her viewpoint, would stretch beyond packing and unpacking. Opportunities such as this are relational goldmines or landmines depending on one's course of action. Fortunately, Brian came around. The memory of the "Move of 2010" has joined an ever-growing collection of showdowns and meltdowns we Fishers choose to laugh about as we continue learning to live and love together as a family.

Responses of believers to the Father's plans aren't all that different. The temptation to speed up or take control of these sacred plans as He moves us along in the working out of our salvation is great. While it can be easy to embrace the big picture of our salvation, the details offer lots of opportunity for derailment. Trouble comes because we're prone to reacting to our own perspectives, or we're influenced by ulterior motives.

While we've been given the gift of new life, including sanctity and the restoration of our dignity, the stage is set for opposing forces as real as Brian and Georgia's conflict that morning. Our responses to these clashing principles say much about our hearts as well as our willingness or ability to trust our Restorer.

God's plan is to move us ever-deeper into this new and glorious life made possible in Christ. This life frees us to receive and give love. And while that sounds like something we should desire, the truth is, we're not always sure we want to follow this exact plan.

Often, we have different ideas, or we aren't convinced such an existence is possible. We're unwilling to wrestle with our weaknesses, we're too ashamed, or we don't know how to engage in the work. Of course, we can't admit to any of these tendencies, not to anyone; not even to ourselves sometimes. What would people think if they knew of our reluctance? What would we do if we dared be that honest with ourselves?

Ironically, the very road to freedom often finds us choosing or defaulting to disgrace. The fear of this degree of vulnerability and being divinely known drives us into seclusion. It causes us to withhold parts of our needy hearts from the Father. We fail to pursue the depths of redemption available to us. In our quest to survive, we don't hear or sometimes perhaps we remain unmoved as the Father speaks and sings His tender heart toward us; and we get in our own way of allowing Him to move us along in this transforming journey.

Instead, we busy ourselves with devising a different plan than His. Our plan seems good enough, seems like it could bring fulfillment even as it's carried out with our own sweat equity. In reality, we're erecting barriers around our hearts to ourselves, to others, and most important, to our Creator. Our alternative plans lack the powerful influence and imagination of the all-knowing and righteous One. What's more, without God's empowering grace, our results fall pitifully short in accomplishing glorious possibilities we've not dreamed of.

During Jesus' earthly ministry, the disciples had been closer to Him than anyone. They'd listened to Him, eaten with Him, laughed with Him, and talked with Him. Beyond that, they allowed Him to know them, even when their mortal hearts betrayed their best intentions.

After the ascension, the disciples entered the post-resurrection era, eventually gaining the attention of their world. Modern-day places like Jerusalem and the West Bank, portions of Africa and the Middle East, areas in Greece, Rome and other regions actually witnessed Christ through these men[1].

It's important to understand how the disciples successfully communicated Christ. It wasn't their access to resources. It wasn't that they solved every problem or filled every need. It wasn't their social status or excellent oratory skills. It wasn't their ability to get things done or their commitment to any church-led missions initiative. It was their passion that drove them. They were the beneficiaries of transforming relationship with none other than Emmanuel Himself. It was an ongoing gift they couldn't help but share, because it was their very lives.

I'm guessing they didn't realize while it was happening, but as the days turned to weeks, then months and years, the Son of God taught, exposed, forgave, and inspired them, then through the overcoming power of the cross and the resurrection, by the power of God's Spirit, He empowered men that had once been merely fishermen and debt collectors to accomplish God kinds of things. Gradually, as they gained an unshakeable trust in Him, these men surrendered their hearts, minds, wants, needs, strengths and weaknesses to the One who is faithful.

On the day of Pentecost, almost two full months after Jesus' ascension to the Father, surely most of the residents of Jerusalem had gotten past the troubling case of Jesus. All the religious and political uneasiness He'd caused, as well as all those rumors of miracles that just couldn't be, it was all history now. Yet, out of nowhere, a spectacle began to unfold, drawing the attention of a gathering crowd there outside the Upper Room.

There was a sound like rushing wind, yet the air around them remained still. The rustling came from inside the quarters, where the disciples had gathered. What were these religious fellows up to? Visitors to the city for that annual Holy Day sensed something inexplicable happening, as Spirit-filled Christ-followers descended from their meeting place.

By day's end, everyone in attendance, regardless of race or background, encountered God, as the testimony of Peter and the others revealed individuals who'd become transformed men. The change within them was an astounding God-force that moved them, out of that room where they'd gathered, and out of the comfort of their routine. These were finally men who were becoming, fully engaged and alive in their faith. Their resulting strength and wisdom was more than infectious.

This scene wasn't just a gathering of people. Numbered among those in attendance that day was God Himself. Working to fulfill His plan, God poured out His Spirit in the hearts of seekers of God who'd been gathering at these annual festivals for years. On that day, His Spirit tendered the hearts of those spectators to see the reality that they were lost wanderers in need of rescue. It was His Spirit who gifted men, women, and children with the faith to believe their true and glorious lives could be found in the salvation only Jesus had the power and authority to offer.

And it was the authenticity of relationship developing between the disciples and the Jesus they proclaimed that made them credible witnesses of the good news of Christ. A divine partnership. How far they'd come from their well-chronicled days of wandering off course! They were now trustworthy vessels that Almighty God could trust to minister alongside His Spirit to those in need.

Another of God's chosen, the Apostle Paul, would discover the wonder of this divine plan as well. This was a man who became so full of God that he once reacted to a poisonous snake bite by casually shaking the deadly serpent, which was latched onto his hand, into a burning fire while he himself remained unharmed. God did extraordinary miracles through Paul on numerous occasions, yet in spite of all the achievements and influence of his evangelistic ministry, Paul became bothered by a painful thorn, which it has been suggested, felt similar to a fist repeatedly striking his rib cage.

Sounds uncomfortable to me. Considering his miracle-filled history, I'm guessing he was none too concerned. He'd seen God do the impossible so often, I wonder if he was even surprised anymore. Actually, I wonder if it was more surprising to Paul that God didn't do the miraculous in this instance, as he prayed this troublesome thorn be removed.

With the issue unresolved, Paul asked again, and he heard a sound I've heard and feared in my own prayers with the Father; the sound of nothing, not one word or sign. But Paul's confident relationship with the Father provided all the resilience he needed to keep asking, to continue expecting a divine answer.

It took three of these one-sided conversations before God chose to reply to Paul, yet, I wonder because of his familiarity with God's faithfulness, if the intensity with which Paul waited and listened wasn't growing stronger with each one-sided exchange. Sometimes silence can work wonders in gaining a captive audience. However, when God did speak, it was hardly what Paul had asked for:

> My grace is enough; it's all you need.
> My strength comes into its own in your weakness.
> (2 Corinthians 12:9, The Message)

As much as anything, it's Paul's reaction to this surprising response that interests me. In describing this divine answer to his friends at Corinth, Paul's words were dripping with enthusiasm. This is somewhat surprising, considering Paul was going to have to continue enduring something akin to his ribcage tolerating the pain of an uninvited wooden stake.

But Paul knew what it was to follow hard after a man-made plan. He'd been one of those religious sorts who had no room in his heart for the Spirit to inform and instruct him. He'd been certain he was right, too, until he had his own encounter with truth and love; and mercy. To that time, Paul had been strong, but flawed. Through eyes that had finally seen grace, Paul realized his strength was meaningless. It was a lesson that must have been painful, as he realized the damage he'd inflicted with all his good intentions and in the name of his religious notions.

But that was then, before he became the Apostle Paul. This latest thorny setback was in the midst of a God-filled life. Why would Paul need any hindrance to what he'd now become? Paul understood he was on a journey. He'd seen and come to know enough of God's grace that he'd gladly embrace the reality that his earthly existence would always be limited, that there would always be flaws of some kind to address. That thorn was a welcome reminder for him to continue carrying these realities right up to the throne of Almighty God so that the process of his transformation could continue from glory to ever-increasing glory.

This is the way to true strength, God's strength. The humility, resiliency, and hunger that Paul demonstrates in submitting to God's grace and embracing God's strength is what delivered Paul from the shackles of the persecutor's life—wrong about everything he lived for, to the heights of distinction and honor as a hero—having shared in the labor of God's ongoing search and rescue work within our world. And it is our ticket out of lives of insignificance and futility as well.

As with these early apostles' lives, God wants us to be free to live healthy, whole, and fulfilling lives, but the truth is, by nature we're prone to living in our own strength, even as believers. Through the redeemed life of Paul and the disciples' role during the birthing of the very church that we belong to, we get a taste of the greater realities available to us as we surrender our plans to God. But have we considered the repercussions when we limit God's influence and presence in our lives?

With the poorly chosen path I followed for so long, I glimpsed the impact it had on my relationships and my sense of self. It led me to such despair that I eventually abandoned my plan in favor of God's. And then I had Joe and witnessed from a different perspective the hollow and even worse, harmful effect of our self-determined plans.

I saw how even the noblest of intentions can harm, how believers on a mission to do great things can fail to grasp the greatest needs. Why? Because of unsurrendered agendas. Many search for ways to use their faith; unfortunately, their intention is to use it for their own survival and gain, even if they aren't aware of these tendencies. Such pitfalls have contributed to an unhealthy and disjointed Body.

We've been called into relationship with Emanuel as the disciples were, to allow Him into the depths of our lives as they did; to be transformed by that relationship just like them. It's hard to argue with the results. Their lives took on significance and relevancy they could never have earned on their own as they assisted God Himself in the establishment of the very church that lives today.

When their earthly journey gave way to the full realization of eternal glory, this mantle of faith was prayerfully passed down through the generations. It's available to us even now. But so much time has passed, and in all honesty, we've settled into our own routines.

God often brings opportunities for us to see the cold, uncomfortable truth, often through people like Joe. And more often than not, the truth is, we lack authenticity. We lack integrity. Quite frankly, we lack humility! And we tend to live out of our own strength while avoiding or denying these realities.

We busy ourselves with things to do—even good Christian activities, and we stay stuck. It isn't that God is surprised or angry at our shortcomings. It's just that as long as we keep ignoring these life-draining tendencies, we limit what He can do about them. We limit what He can do in us and through us; and we remain victims of a lost glory.

During a family vacation to northwestern Michigan, we took a day to explore the sights of the Upper Peninsula. We also crossed over the International Bridge into Sault Ste. Marie, Ontario. We had little time to linger on the Canadian side of I-75 since we'd already spent several hours exploring many of the stunning views along the way. It was my first time to travel so far north; it was a first, going through customs. It was my first time to set foot on foreign soil. And it was the first time I ever heard of a regional food called pierogis.

The sun hung low in the sky as we exited the highway to a promising restaurant situated off Lake Huron. We planned to have a quick meal before heading back. Once seated and full of enthusiasm, I asked our server what I thought to be a simple question, "Can you tell me what a pierogi is?" It was right there on the board, listed as 'Special of the Day: Deep-Fried Pierogis."

I was intrigued. Being a true Southerner, I understood the deep-fried part. However, even if it was Canada, it was a foreign country. I wasn't interested in partaking of deep-fried anything if I didn't have a clue what it was.

Our waitress, a reserved woman who spoke with a fancy accent, answered, "Well, it's a pierogi."

I don't know about you, but I was taught to never define a word using that word. Not only had she broken this important rule, she didn't use any adjectives that might provide the slightest clue of what this mystery menu item might be.

Of course, I'm not one to give up easily, so I pressed for more. However, it seemed the more I asked, the less she offered on the subject. If anything was becoming clear, it was that the Fisher family would be leaving Canada without the slightest inkling of what a pierogi was. I suppose that's progress because before that evening, I didn't even know there was such a thing.

The point is, how can we as believers truly function if we don't realize how vital it is for God to show up in our stories? For Him to meet us where we are as undone, lost, and confused so He can fill us with meaning and purpose? For Him to get us back on course and work out the pride that so easily separates us from His grace?

If we aren't coming to know Him in those places, how can we follow in the disciples' footsteps? How can we offer our world authentic glimpses of a God we're not all that intimately acquainted with? How can God's strength come into its own within and around us? How can we gain the confidence and resiliency of Paul when we encounter our own awkward spiritual silences?

Heaven forbid we leave those we encounter with no better inkling of the true nature of Christ than that waitress left me with those Canadian pierogis. God's grace is sufficient. And this Truth, as it begins to penetrate our self-sufficient and prideful tendencies, is a Truth worth living for.

April 4, 2007

FAMILY'S LOSS IS NO ONE'S GAIN

By CARRIE BULLOCK FISHER

REELING FROM RECENT charges, a local family is trying to rise above the increased media and legal scrutiny they now face.

The family was once hailed for their generosity to the community, but there is growing evidence that many within the family are now looking out for their own interests.

As pressure mounts from an exhaustive investigation, attention is now turning to the vast amount of resources at the family's disposal and exactly how they are being used. The family business has been a major source of worldwide fruit production and has suffered significant losses of late.

Given the depth of this growing case, many are wondering if the family's longstanding reputation, as well as their much-needed fruit harvests, will ever recover.

Stay tuned for updates on this story as the investigation continues.

Question: Is atheism and agnosticism growing
             in America?
Answer: Yes, because god (sic) has not shown
             us anything for a while.
Answer: I sure hope so. What's been leading
             The way so far ain't working to (sic)
             good!
Answer: If it was growing in scope, it would
             Likely be due to a fundamental
             Disparity between how religious
             people talk . . . and then behave.
                            ALL ANONYMOUS
             (THE ANSWER BAG, WORLD WIDE WEB)

     Therefore, . . . let us throw off everything
   that hinders and the sin that so easily entangles,
       and let us run with perseverance the race
          marked out for us. Let us fix our eyes
       on Jesus, the author and perfecter of our faith,
    . . . and do not lose heart when He rebukes you.
                         (HEBREWS 12:1, 2A, 5B)

When Joe was a newborn, we lived near the foothills of the Blue Ridge Mountains. This was a far cry from the gently sloping hills I was raised on. In our new home situated in the shadow of the mountains, there was almost always a stiff breeze which I never got used to. This was a small price to pay, however, in light of the beauty all around me. As often as possible I would gather up little baby Joe, and together, we'd head out to explore the nooks and crannies of this magnificent landscape.

One particular fall morning, we discovered a little country road framed by sun-soaked open-pasture fields on either side. The driving was easy until the straight and flat asphalt gave way to a sudden hair-pin turn that obscured the view of what lay ahead. As I approached the sharp curve, I spotted an orchard and thought it might be nice to stop for some apples on our way home. Fall apples are tasty on their own, but are even better when tossed with sugar, butter, and cinnamon, then wrapped in a flaky crust for frying.

Dinner plans made, well at least for the dessert portion of the meal, I drove on. Past the orchard, the pale hue of open pasture gave way to the brilliance of fall leaves shimmering in a grove of trees. Just off the road in a small clearing was a little brick church.

I turned the car into a gravel parking lot, crushed rock crackling as the tires rolled to a stop. There was a weathered outhouse to the rear and a shaded cemetery on the far side of the church. The whole scene reminded me of the little country churches my family used to sing at when I was growing up, a comforting thought since I'd been homesick ever since we moved so far away.

Fallen leaves covered the entire property, even the roof of the church. The leaves with their varying colors on the ground made a thick-piled carpet begging to be walked on. A few precious streams of sunlight peeked through any nook and cranny they could find, dancing merrily at their breakthrough. The only discernible sounds were the leaves rattling softly in the breeze and the birds cooing and singing overhead as they fluttered about. It was a wonderland, a magical place that I enjoyed so much, I had to get Brian to see this enchanted scene. It was a drive we repeated on several occasions.

Beautiful as it was, this little church with all its charm and serenity was a deserted place. The grounds were maintained and the building seemed in modern condition, but not once did I encounter anyone there.

Much time has passed since those carefree days for Joe and me. Extreme hairpin turns have yielded to erratic emotions that overtake Joe with little to no notice. Inviting views are threatened by waves of volatility which must be carefully negotiated to minimize their destructive force. In this journey I've often recalled that deserted church, for I have discovered a similar feeling of isolating emptiness.

As Joe entered his high school years, Brian and I placed him in a special school where we hoped he'd fit in. Joe had grown into a six foot plus young man with a solid frame, so he was recruited to join the school basketball team. It was a team that rarely won a ballgame, yet the guys were thrilled just to play. With their disabilities, they knew they'd never have a chance at playing on a more competitive team.

For three years I travelled to home and away games and watched with growing disappointment at how the team fared against their competitors. Since there were no other schools with similarly challenged teams, they played in a conference made up of mostly Christian schools. Playing each team multiple times each year, we came to know our opposition fairly well. In turn they knew they could go ahead and mark the "W" when our names came up on the schedule.

Amidst the cloud of losing, our boys always put on a brave front. They treated their opponents with respect and played as hard as they could. While our school wasn't a Christian-based school, the guys knew and respected the other teams' religious rituals including team prayers. But with each game, our team also knew what was in store; a long night of teasing, harassment and intimidation along with another thorough beat-down.

Although they suffered significant losses, sometimes more than forty to fifty points, it wasn't the losing that broke my heart. There was an even deeper loss.

Game after game, team by team, I saw Christians in the stands, on the sidelines, and on the court, miss the most important goal. These were brothers and sisters who were intent on their mission of winning, yet their eyes failed to peer into our sons' eyes, and their hearts never envisioned the greater possibilities within their grasp.

Instead of recognizing the opportunity before them, they embraced an inferior goal by living out a perceived Christian excellence, a dedication to performance that came at the price of exploiting the weaknesses of our sons.

Missing this important goal isn't just occurring in Christian athletics, however. And it isn't just the mentally ill who pay the price. If I've learned anything here in this valley, it's that even followers of Christ are prone to judge instead of discern. We're vulnerable to arrogance, and we often busy ourselves with the particulars to the point that we miss the bigger picture.

Even the disciples weren't immune from these tendencies. Jesus called these, His closest followers, to work alongside Him on behalf of the Kingdom. Through Him, they were authorized and became empowered to minister to those in need.

This new calling was a real promotion from their previous discipleship responsibilities, which had probably consisted of securing food, resources, and making arrangements for their group as they travelled through Galilee and beyond; important work, to be sure, but there were greater works to do.

These men were becoming more than just hearers of the Word. They were, by God's grace, becoming ministers of the Gospel. Unbelievably, evil spirits departed at these disciples' God-infused command. Diseases were negated. The good news of the Kingdom was communicated, and in their midst, many minds, hearts, and bodies were restored to their true and sound state.

God had seen fit to entrust these fickle-hearted mortals with His divine glory, yet even as the disciples must have swelled with excitement at the work they were doing, an argument broke out. From the heights of divine inspiration to the depths of pride and insecurity, Jesus' apprentices began feuding with one another over who was the greatest disciple; in public—with children present!

Twelve determined minds full of reasons and justifications as to why each man felt certain he was deserving of this distinction. If Jesus hadn't interrupted, I'm betting the situation would've turned even uglier.

There's no indication that Jesus was angered by the disciples' arrogance, or that He tried to hide this little setback from those in attendance. As He reached out to a child who'd been watching nearby, I imagine the disciples began to fidget a bit. I say this because every time children attempted to approach Jesus, the disciples tried to shoo them away as if they were a nuisance, unworthy of Jesus' time or attention. Of course, every time the disciples shooed them away, Jesus blew their minds by not only welcoming these little perceived distractions—He relished interacting with them.

But back to this most recent crisis. Of all the things Jesus could've said or done, He chose to honor someone perceived as a waste of time, the very people His followers seemed to devalue the most. It must've been an incredible challenge for these men who adored Jesus. In one simple gesture, He'd shown they were much further from greatness than they imagined, yet He didn't shame them, and they didn't lose heart. This is what it was to work out their salvation, step by step, victory by victory, and even setback by setback.

On the heels of this humbling incident, the very next conversation recorded in Scripture illustrated how great their need continued to be. It was John who said,

> . . . we saw someone driving out demons in
> your name, and we tried to stop him, because
> he is not one of us. (Luke 9:49)

It was yet another opportunity for Jesus to shed light on their hearts and to grow them beyond the destructive forces of their thoughts and tendencies.

These first men of faith weren't all that different from us. We struggle with our own modern-day arrogance, are prone to overlooking those we can't fix or relate to, and we tend to look down on or mistrust others whose faith walk doesn't fit neatly into our version of what it should be.

Thankfully, Jesus is still patiently confronting us, still inviting us to keep up the good work of salvation within us, yet there are signs that we tenders of the faith in this generation lack much of an authentic spiritual presence;

evidences that we're missing Him, that we've gotten off course, and that we've settled into a form of Christianity that lacks an elemental essence of Christlikeness.

So God sends us Joe and countless others. He offers us opportunities to see our sin, to work out our salvation, to deepen our faith. God has placed a portion of His glory in Joe, and in others who languish as the "least of these." To look past them, as we're prone to do, is to look away from God. It brings to light a troubling reality; we would choose which parts of God we embrace and which we choose not to embrace. In doing so, we limit the effect of His grace and empowering in our lives.

> . . . by the grace of God I am what I am,
> and His grace to me was not without effect.
> (1 Corinthians 15:10)

What if Paul hadn't become the Apostle? What if he had his moment with God on that road to Damascus, then decided to devote the rest of his life to living for God? But what if he chose to do so while holding onto a few things? Perhaps pride? Or maybe his superior thinking and reasoning skills? What if he'd allowed the thorn to have the final say?

Paul was quite brilliant and persuasive, so I believe his charisma alone would've convinced some to join him in his allegiance to the faith. But troubling repercussions were sure to come should Paul have chosen this alternative plan:

- his converts would've been influenced by the limited and unfulfilling existence we're pretending Paul might've settled for, and
- in spite of Paul's influential gifting, this unfulfilled potential would've limited God's ability to work in and through him, reducing the impact of his labor

by a staggering amount; instead of being known as an apostle, it's likely he would have been known more as Paul the Opinionated.

Thankfully, there are no 'what if's' where Paul is concerned. But there is sobering evidence that the 'what if' scenario has crept into the present. Followers of Christ have been assigned the task of The Great Commission, yet the logistical challenges of this proclamation are huge. Even when Jesus appointed the disciples for this task at Mt. Olivet, the world population is estimated to have been somewhere between one-hundred-fifty million to six-hundred million people. Jesus was speaking to a mere eleven men at the time!

Our planet's population has now exploded to almost seven billion people. Instead of making headway, Christians are striking out in their evangelistic efforts. Statistics fuel studies showing the Church is losing ground. Membership is down within local churches. Baptisms are down. Giving is down. And most telling, people are disillusioned at our watered-down version of faith.

Surely our hearts should skip a few beats upon the realization of our beleaguered state. We're failing globally, locally. Why? Because we've not effectively communicated the good news of the Kingdom. We've obscured the message. Most people don't want to be chided for their honest struggle with difficult problems or to be dismissed in the midst of excruciating uncertainties with a cold reminder of God's faithfulness. They don't want to be invited to a new Sunday school class or a different church by someone who believes this is the answer to their problems. And they don't want to be trampled on by those in pursuit of "excellence."

These ministering strategies are far more common than they should be. I know because here in this valley of suffering

I've encountered them countless times. And I've watched as others have endured the indignity of this kind of ministry as well.

People don't feel honored as God's chosen when presented with a heartless Gospel. Our self-inspired efforts and good intentions are but a drop in the bucket in among such brokenness. What this world needs is to see evidence of Emmanuel . . . God with us. They need grace, the divine empowering to be and do more than their mortal flesh allows.

We in the Body of Christ also need a growing knowledge of the kind of grace that made Paul what he became, the apostle. We must become hungry for God's enabling power which allows us to embrace our own weaknesses and limitations. And we must become desperate for experiential knowledge of Emmanuel and His sustaining and healing power within us, as those early disciples were. Because the world doesn't need more salesmen or reformers or opinionated pursuers of excellence. It needs to be shown the effect of grace, our greatest resource. What better way than for it to be evident in us?

Part of the joy of mothering, for me, has been cooking and baking for my family. Over the years, Joe and Georgia have latched onto a few favorite dishes. Now that Georgia is cooking more for herself, she's trying to replicate some of her favorites. Unfortunately, she isn't always satisfied with the results of her efforts.

Of course, I want her to enjoy baking. I can imagine a time when she'll be baking for her own children, and I want her to feel the same joy I've felt. So when her baking falls short of her expectations, we'll head to the kitchen to see if we can pinpoint the problem.

Armed with a glass of tea for me and a bottle of water for her, we'll sit at the table that has seen her grow from an infant into a beautiful young lady. Looking over the recipe, we check to see if she omitted an ingredient or failed to carry out a step. More often than not, she's done as the recipe instructs.

Right about this time she'll get a look of despair on her face, the one that tugs at a mother's heart. As I rush to soothe her discouragement, I put an arm around her and draw her close. Then I ask, "Did you remember the secret ingredient?"

It's a bit of an inside joke that originated from Brian's childhood. His mother, who's an excellent cook, had a penchant for stashing surprise ingredients in the foods she cooked. When the meal was over, she'd ask her family, "Can you guess the secret ingredient?"

Brian wasn't always thrilled when he learned what he'd just eaten. He liked to know when he was eating zucchini and preferred that it look like zucchini. He favored meat purchased from a grocery store. He was particularly squeamish about the cheese when it unexpectedly gushed out of his hot dog. He did, however, enjoy the rhubarb pared with strawberries and pastry in what came to be his favorite pie.

Once grown and with kids of his own, Brian would share stories around our dinner table about these secret ingredients from his past. Joe and Georgia got the biggest kick out of hearing them. Of course, I had three sets of eyes determined to make sure I didn't follow in my mother-in-law's footsteps.

With all this scrutiny, the only secret ingredient I could ever get away with adding was love. It was an ingredient I tried to use liberally though. Planning around everyone's tastes as best I could while preparing wholesome meals was challenging at times, but it was a way for me to show my love, and I think they recognized it.

In some hard-to-explain way, when Georgia eats something I've cooked, whether it's something as simple as a bowl of oatmeal or a warm cherry pie, it evokes memories of bowls of oatmeal and fruit pies I've prepared for her through the years. While savoring the present she's also reminded of times past. Every bite is a constant reminder and reinforcement of my love and favor toward her.

That's what she wants to recreate, not just a baked good prepared by following a handed-down recipe, but those cherished feelings of love and favor. Even though it may nourish her body, she's looking for something that nourishes her soul with that same infusion of devotion and care.

That's similar to what grace should be like. It's the secret ingredient that has the potential to infuse the way we live our lives. As we allow God's grace to penetrate the depths of our hearts—failure by failure, hurt by hurt, thorn by thorn—we find we're being restored in the knowledge of God's love and favor to the depths of our being. It's a force so compelling and contagious, it becomes the sweet fragrance of Christ within us, if we can find the courage to make ourselves available to it.

If we don't have a growing familiarity of this secret ingredient that is grace, no matter what other ingredients or strategies we rely on, our efforts will always fall short.

Whether our interests lead us into political reformation, church growth, or even something as simple as competing in a simple sporting event, we have much opportunity. The eyes of the world are looking for God in us.

What if those within the realm of our influence had been standing outside the Upper Room on the day of Pentecost? As the disciples emerged on the scene, full of the Holy Spirit, what would these time-travelers have seen and heard? Doubters accused the disciples of being nothing more than a bunch of drunks, yet a sober-minded Peter, along with the remainder of the disciples, encouraged and compelled by God's conspicuous presence, embraced this work of grace.

Something real and significant happened that day. A mind-boggling three-thousand people began their own journey of faith.

Of course there's no time-travelling option here. The hurting and wounded of our generation are still waiting to find something to hope for, waiting for the fulfillment that can only come through partaking of our secret ingredient.

And we still have this Great Commission that awaits fulfillment. Most of our present strategies are proving ineffective. The fact is, there was something supernatural occurring within and through these earliest evangelical efforts; not political, not circumstantial, not man-made. The way to aid in providing what the world desperately needs is to submit our plans, motives, strategies, and most of all, our hearts to the One capable of fulfilling His glorious plans in and through us, as He did the disciples.

Until we followers of Christ submit our hearts more fully to God's grace, we'll lack the very heart that defines the Body of Christ. We mustn't settle for the sense of community our local church participation provides or feelings of accomplishment from our acts of service that seem to be Christ-worthy. We must not attempt to limit God's work within us, not if we're to rise up and embrace this gloriously divine plan that far exceeds our own.

Can we fail to know the depth of our identity in Christ and still save the world? "For you know the grace of our Lord Jesus Christ," the Apostle Paul declared to the Corinthians. "I consider everything a loss compared to the surpassing greatness of knowing Christ Jesus my Lord," he proclaimed to his dearly loved friends at Philippi.

Oh, to have this degree of familiarity, this level of passion. It's what we desperately need. Without it, we aren't all that different from that abandoned church I happened upon such a long time ago, giving the appearance of something glorious but lacking the depth of heart that enables us to offer a real presence in the valleys of this world.

May we continue to pursue knowing and making use of this grace, so that our best days are not all the way back at Pentecost. In due time, we, too, stand to see a move of God like we can't imagine.

FAMILY RECOVERS NAME, LONG LOST FORTUNE

By CARRIE BULLOCK FISHER

AN AREA FAMILY IS ENJOYING renewed success as the beneficiaries of what was a lost fortune.

The family, who became mired in several scandals, has reclaimed its good-standing in the community after suffering significant personal as well as professional setbacks. Many left their homes on the family complex behind.

To cover rising costs, they mortgaged many individually held properties, eventually losing them in foreclosure.

The family business, a major worldwide fruit supplier, almost failed, causing a serious shortage for consumers.

Several family members were ridiculed as their losses mounted. Others lost touch. Many turned on one another.

Their fortunes began to change when several of the estranged family members sought help from the family patriarch.

The Father, apparently undeterred by the course of events, had preserved the family's business and estate. After paying off their debts and settling their legal issues, the Father appointed them as executives over the family business.

Now the eyes of the world are on them as they prepare to forge ahead.

Praise the LORD, O my soul; all my inmost being,
praise His holy name. Praise the LORD,
O my soul, and forget not all His benefits-
who forgives all your sins and heals all your
diseases, who redeems your life from the pit and
crowns you with love and compassion, who satisfies
your desires with good things so that your youth
is renewed like the eagle's. The LORD works
righteousness and justice for all the oppressed . . .
The LORD is compassionate and gracious, slow to
anger, abounding in love.
KING DAVID (PSALM 103:1-6, 8)

During freshman year at college, my roommate decided to throw a surprise party to celebrate my birthday. Naturally, there was a great deal of secrecy leading up to the big event. Unfortunately, all that mystery exacerbated my ongoing insecurities. I feared that her increased busyness and secret-keeping confirmed what I was sure I already knew; she'd grown weary of being my friend.

While she worked to bless me, I simmered and stewed over my perceived notions of a failed friendship. The consequences of my insecurities were undeniable. My distrust fueled the way I treated a dear friend, leaving her hurt. For me, the benefits of our friendship went largely unrealized because of the hidden fears of my heart. Finding myself the honored guest of my friend's planned surprise, there seemed little to celebrate. I felt I'd lost her respect. I'd certainly lost mine . . . what little I had anyway.

Not everyone deals with this degree of insecurity. However, reaping the benefits of relationship to a God we don't completely comprehend is challenging. Yet we're desperate to know these very benefits; not just in knowing about them intellectually, but knowing them experientially. Like the magic of a first kiss, a mother's thrill of holding her newborn child, or the exhilaration of watching the sun set over shimmering waters or soaring mountain peaks. These kinds of experiences move us, which is good because we were made to be moved. Hearts touched by God's love and His glorious magnificence are genuinely moved, transformed bit by bit.

King David was moved and awestruck by this God with whom he fell more in love with as God's own love penetrated deeper and deeper within his being. The Amplified Bible says David sought to bless God with "all that was deepest" within him.

He wasn't alone. Joining in the celebration of transforming love were the disciples who soon followed. They outgrew fears, pride, and even their insecurities. They overcame disappointments, loneliness, and a world of other wounds. They persevered through the many difficulties they encountered in a hostile world. And they learned to identify and resist the lies and schemes of the enemy, all this as divine glory became evident in them. They dared embark upon their journey of faith, and in so doing, they discovered a quality of life that resonated down to their very essence.

The Bible provides us with a beautiful glimpse of these men who loved God with hearts, minds, and souls fully engaged in divine transformation, yet there's a quality about this love that we must not overlook; their love was a reaction. As John the Apostle proclaimed a millennium after King David's life, "We love, because He first loved us." These men were well-acquainted with God's love. And they flourished as a result of the benefits that came about because of that love.

Followers of Christ in this generation have the same opportunity to respond to this transforming love, to grow beyond where we are, to overcome and persevere; to learn to recognize where the enemy has subdued or sabotaged God's good intentions toward us. We have the opportunity to embark upon our own unique journey of faith and to discover a deeper capacity for joy, love and life.

It's in this place of reaction we can begin to live out the call that God has given the Body of Christ, to love God with all that we are, to love ourselves in an ever-maturing way, and to love those who come into our paths. Given the scope of these greatest of all of God's instructions to us, we also have the freedom to recognize we're merely growing in this Christlike love. Bumps and hiccups will come because we're not yet complete.

Our paths will inevitably turn up those who seem unlovely. Along the way, our limitations will undoubtedly reveal themselves, yet what if we viewed these setbacks as reminders to embrace the gift of humility? And opportunities to discover more life within us in this great faith-adventure?

Jesus knew the disciples weren't ready. The enormity of the task of establishing an enduring Church was clearly beyond their capabilities, yet He continued pouring Himself into them anyway, never wavering from preparing them for this grandiose task; so many obstacles, such frail hearts. But

Jesus showed no signs of regret over choosing these inconsistent men.

There was no condemnation, even as they argued over who was the better man. It was important to Jesus that these men understand He'd never shame them. He understood the frailty of their condition, the valleys they'd wandered for so long, and the limitations of their reasoning.

But He also knew their hearts. These were men who'd chosen Jesus over every single worldly possession, relationship, or pursuit they'd ever known. And He understood it was a divine gift of faith enabling them to believe what their minds couldn't even begin to make sense of. It was a holy anointing that chose them before they ever dreamed of choosing such a journey. Jesus knew God was willing and able to accomplish every single God-sized task and overcome every God-sized obstacle.

Jesus knew His disciples' intentions as well. They were loyal and hungry to know an existence beyond what they could eke out on their own. But Jesus not only invested in them; He relished being with them. As astounding as it seems, He genuinely loved these men.

Yes, He instructed them, but they chose to cherish His instruction even as they sensed His affections toward them. Yes, He asked much of them, but they grasped that the smallness of their thinking combined with their limited human potential was nothing compared to the glorious hope of life available to them in Christ.

Even when they didn't understand, they came to trust. Why? Because they got to know this Man who was their Messiah. They knew He was their salvation. They'd seen the miracles. Peter, James, and John had even heard God Himself confirm that Jesus was the Son of God!

When John approached Jesus to confess the disciples had tried to stop others from doing the work of God, it's telling that they hadn't asked Jesus about this before. Even as John explained the situation to Jesus, he wasn't asking for guidance. I get the feeling John had gone back to fishing in the hope that Jesus would approve of their actions.

But in Jesus, there was still no indication of anger or despair at how tedious the process of sanctification was for the disciples. There was only His redirecting their hearts toward truth and faith. Don't think the disciples didn't notice their self-indulgent natures being shot down at every turn, yet still they followed, and listened, embraced, and became men of faith, not divided by their self-absorbed tendencies nor diminished by their self-reliant schemes nor bound by their human condition.

This is the opportunity we have. Empowered by our growing familiarity with God's love for us, we have the grand opportunity to react to that reality; genuine and enthusiastic love for our Redeemer for starters. We're the beneficiaries of choice. We're no longer doomed to our faithless ways of living and perceiving, but as the disciples ebbed and flowed in this great journey, so do we. The call to love isn't an easy one. It costs everything we've invested in as we've searched for fulfillment and settled for a lesser existence.

As Jesus did with the disciples, He longs to pour into our hearts and lives. We've been charged with participating in the ongoing work of a connected Body, the very church the disciples established in love and by faith. The body of evidence suggests we struggle with some of the same faithless tendencies that plagued the disciples' immature faith.

For instance, did you know we've inherited a religious system consisting of over 38,000 denominations[1]? It's true that there are different visions and giftings. No one group of people could ever touch the depth or breadth of who God is. It's the diversity of humanity working together in loving faith that best reveals Almighty God, yet instead of becoming one Body, our differences have served as dividers.

As surely as arms, legs, eyes, and ears combine to provide our physical bodies with the ability to move and to function, we need our differences to function as the Body we've been ordained to be. The challenge we face is learning to grow and move together in the midst of our differentness.

Instead of differing traditions and denominations excluding one another, and us limiting our associations to those who don't threaten our sense of comfort, we as the church need to cultivate an enthusiasm for discovering more of God in our differentness.

Division is not a natural development that has occurred within the fabric of the Church. It's pride and arrogance that's largely gone unchecked. It's a technologically enabled and culturally sophisticated reenactment of the very condemnation the disciples kept reverting to. Oh that we would contemplate Jesus' response to John in addressing our own tendencies:

> . . . we saw someone driving out demons
> in your name, and we tried to stop him,
> because he is not one of us. (Luke 9:49)

> "Do not stop [withhold, deny or refuse anything to]
> him," Jesus said. "For no one who does a miracle
> in my name can in the next moment
> say anything bad about me." (Mark 9:39)

This is a powerful and challenging response Jesus delivers. First of all, it begs the question, am I actually doing anything miraculous in Jesus' name, something beyond action-items powered by my overactive but limited imagination and usually chock full of self-absorbed ambition?

But then Jesus challenges us to consider the works of others who proclaim the Name of Jesus. Are they doing God things? Not the things we think they should be doing, not things we can explain or understand necessarily, but God things? And, you know, the way to discern either of these questions is by doing what John finally did—by going to the source, Jesus Himself.

"For he who is not against us is for us,[2]" Jesus tells John. Really? This should be a game-changer shouldn't it? No matter our differences?

If we're going to rise up and fulfill our call as one connected Body of Christ, we need the overcoming authority of the One and Only to draw us to a place of unity and connectedness.

It's time for us to discern what our established church traditions and denominational choices are and what they are not. I fear that for many, these very traditions and choices have become idolatrous. It will take a growing faith to overcome the mountain of differences that keep us from fulfilling the call to love.

What are some of the distractions that hinder us in the journey of becoming, or that keep us separate? It could be our everyday choices. How we handle our resources; how we invest our time, or even how we live out our Christian values.

Each facet of our lives presents the opportunity to exercise our free will, yet we tend to settle for what comes naturally. We must understand what comes naturally isn't necessarily a habit of faith. It's not enough to be known as conservative or liberal, generous or miserly, open or closed. It isn't even whether we devote ourselves to religious principles or skeptical uncertainties. Faithless beliefs and reactions become barriers, hindering our ability to relate to God, ourselves and one another.

It could be the expectation that others think and believe as we do. Yet God didn't make us to be the same. Because of the conflicts that can arise from those who are different, we often seek the safety of like-minded others. Settling for groups and communities who don't rock our world too much, we appoint ourselves the task of charting our own course rather than embracing the twists and turns that God chooses to bring; or we tolerate differing viewpoints and beliefs while harboring an air of superiority.

We're vulnerable to hearts that would unfairly discriminate. It's a great challenge, negotiating diversity in things such as personalities, ideas, emotional expression, intellectual capacity, and ambition, even more so when our religious beliefs come into play, yet when such challenges don't move us to humility, we've missed an opportunity.

After Joe limped across the finish line of high school, we made a decision to send him to a specialized therapeutic facility several hundred miles away, where he lived for over a year. The residents of this healing farm, as it was called, were a cross section of people afflicted with serious and persistent mental illness. While some were engaging and seemed somewhat functional, many were despondent and withdrawn. Some looked approachable, and others were clearly confused and seemed disheveled. For the most part, it was quite simple distinguishing the staff from the residents, except for one particular staff member.

He was a master gardener, offering his organic gardening expertise on the farm while also interacting with the residents. His ideas about people were as radical as some of his nontraditional gardening practices. He was an unpretentious man who was far more interested in relating to Joe and the other patients than he was in fitting in with the rest of the staff. Joe became quite fond of this expert gardener. Living so far from home in his compromised mental state, Joe found this man to be a source of comfort during that difficult period.

During my visits there, I had the pleasure of learning more about this friendly gardener. This wasn't his first stint with the "least of these." He'd also invested years in a homeless ministry. As with this current position, he'd chosen to blend in with his homeless friends.

He said he began to notice a pattern when Christians volunteered their services for the homeless people. He discovered these Christian workers tended to talk down to him and treat him somewhat contemptibly. That is, until they realized he was the director of the homeless mission, not one of the victims they'd come to serve. Once enlightened, their behavior toward him changed.

Honestly, it's hard to get away from this reality. We tend to judge and dismiss far too easily, even as we're trying to "help" the very souls we may be holding in contempt! On the other hand, people of position, those capable of funding our causes, those who lend a feeling of authority and prestige along with those who affirm similar beliefs and share like-minded values, are the people we tend to align ourselves with.

Unfortunately, we tend to avoid acknowledging such realities. It seems easier to minimize their existence within our hearts, yet as long as such attitudes go unchecked, we remain unequipped to grow together as one connected Body.

Followers of Christ living in a fallen world can feel the need to fix the world or to come to God's rescue. While I don't mean to suggest that God doesn't call us to take a stand on His behalf at times, I fear that many of us find ourselves defending God and His laws because it seems like something we should do.

Before anything else, we're called to be transformed ourselves. This in and of itself is a life-long task, one that's easy to neglect. Yet with limited insight and resources, we attempt the impossible task of fixing in others what we cannot fix. And as far as defending God's name or reputation, He doesn't need us to come to His defense! He's big enough to handle the sin of the world . . . actually, He already did.

Why do we flounder in fruitless behaviors, subjecting the Body of Christ to growing disintegration? I'd suggest it's because we don't fully grasp what it is to be a follower of Christ. The resulting consequence is that we often end up in a lifestyle of works.

A challenge with learning and choosing to walk by a Spirit infused faith is that one must develop the discipline of being mindful to check in with the Source of our being, as the disciples did so many times. But you know, in all honesty, this can seem tedious and time-consuming. Worse, there's the fear of hearing nothing.

To truly love is to reflect the authenticity that comes about by hearts being infused by the life-giving qualities only available from the living God. It's the freedom to own that we're merely journeying toward Christlikeness. We haven't yet arrived. It's freedom from the pretense of completeness, and it's the gift of humility.

Reacting to God's love enables us to live out the Commission that Christ gave the church. It isn't a mandate in need of fulfillment by our valiant efforts; it's an inevitable benefit we've been asked to receive. There's a world of difference between these two reactions. To receive, we need only to open our hearts to hear what the disciples before us heard; the message of God's Truth, over and over.

God is reaching out to a broken Body. Through of His Word and the Spirit that's willing, we've been invited to participate in a lifelong journey abounding in His empowering. Among these benefits are

- a life that's rich and full, so we can pursue a purposeful existence,
- forgiveness, elevating us over the effects of sin, adversities, and setbacks in our lives,
- healing and restoration from our undone state,
- the rescue and recovery of our true glory,
- satisfaction without worldly striving,
- promises that God Himself keeps,
- wisdom and knowledge,
- compassion from God to us, and for us to extend to others, and
- an awareness of God and His approachable nature.

When David spoke of the benefits he experienced as a result of the divine connection between him and the Father, he spoke as a man God had seen and yet still loved at David's worst. Yet, this broken king possessed a hunger and a dogged trust of God that kept him right where you and I need to be: in a position to receive.

We have an incredible invitation to enter into the courts of humility, and that's a holy place. Yet, it can be tempting to avoid our wounds and broken places. Our pride and insecurity often keep us from them. Yet the truth is, we're all chosen, as David was.

To witness the kind of healing that only God can bring, we must let God be God. And we mustn't let shame, pride, complacency, or fear keep us from facing our own need. These are tools that have proved successful to our enemy far too long.

What's crippling the Body of Christ isn't that we're broken; it's that we've not allowed the Healer to save us from ourselves! Only He can fill the depths of our being. Only He can know how desperate our need is and lift us from this place. Only He can restore the luster of His glory within us, so our sights are set on a reality far more relevant than our physical existence. Only He can bring us into our own in this world, so that our confidence and abilities reflect His presence in us.

And He does it all with a father's pride and a mother's doting, always. The promise of life in Christ is worthy of celebration.

Every day we travel down Jericho Roads, a place Jesus taught about, where a man was attacked, robbed, and then ignored by the religious community, It was a lowly Gentile who finally rescued and cared for the man. We walk among muggers, the victims they harm, and the religious who are too attached to their own agendas.

In all honestly, we may at one point or another take on every one of the identities in that revealing story ourselves; but as we reap the benefits of our Father's salvation, we, too, can rise to meet the need, empowered, full of faith and out of our excess. And we can hear Jesus say, as He's said to those who've gone before us, "What you did for these, you did for Me."

LOCAL GIRL FINDS HER WAY HOME

By CARRIE BULLOCK FISHER

A LOCAL WOMAN RETURNED home as an honored resident today, forty years after gaining notoriety as an abducted child. She was welcomed by family members, including the family patriarch, who was visibly moved at the sight of his long-lost daughter.

The center of a long-running investigation and news story, hers was a case that stretched into three decades before it was resolved.

Her abductor, after committing crimes in multiple states, was eventually tried and convicted on several counts. He awaits sentencing.

The former captive chose to relocate and dropped out of the public eye.

Her homecoming is especially jubilant, since she is returning, not as a victim, but as one overcoming her troubled and curious past. Asked what she drew on to recover from the trauma of being lost and of her subsequent troubles, she said she finally found the faith to trust in her real Father's love.

If the glory of God can be found in the face of Christ,
Where is the face of Christ found?
In the lowly, the sick, and the needy;
But this glory-treasure is renowned.
It is there for the taking, there to enjoy,
There to lift us from this place
Of shame and accusation,
Of limitation and disgrace.

What this glory is to mortal-man,
Can we begin to know?
The strength and power not our own,
Yet gifts the Father bestows.
To the meek and the hungry
And the poor troubled soul-
He lovingly gives more
As He heals and makes us whole

As we seek,
Must we look very far?
Past memories and impressions
And the dark valleys we are
Dying to live, looking to see
If the faith that moves mountains
Can move even me.

-CARRIE BULLOCK FISHER

Almost a decade has passed since Joe was first diagnosed with serious mental illness. In that time Joe has grown into a young man—on the outside, and he longs to be that on the inside, longs to be "normal," as he often says. He seeks to find his way in this life and wonders if things will ever get easier. Rare are the moments when his mind is clear enough to realize it's betrayed him, leaving only glimmers of hope easily forgotten among waves of torment and disappointment.

At present, his moods continue to swing wildly. He's at risk of falling apart at the slightest circumstance. There's a disconnect with feeling appropriate emotional responses. He has body odor. His teeth are deteriorating for lack of care. He's a magnet for disaster, breaking or losing most everything he touches. It's often difficult to tell whether the concerns he feels are valid or manifestations of his delusions. I worry for his safety.

By the time we had a name for Joe's condition, the relationship between him and Georgia had deteriorated significantly. There were so many reasons for them to resent one another, and they seemed aware and fully empowered by them all.

For Georgia, Joe's existence was a burden; one she probably wished would just go away. His behavior was tiresome and could be embarrassing for her as well. And his condition required so much of Brian and me, I'm sure she felt overlooked at times.

On the other hand, Georgia appeared self-absorbed, impatient, and judgmental to Joe. Where he was chronically unprepared for tasks and assignments, she seemed well prepared. While he struggled to earn decent grades, her academic performance was stellar with little effort. Her peers didn't appear bent on humiliating her, as his did to him.

Through his eyes, it seemed that everything she touched turned to gold. I'm certain he felt that, while the world looked to be against him, it was at her fingertips. They argued and fought with a loathing that concerned me.

For me, having children, complicated by Joe's difficulties, brought the realization that the intensive labor begins after the kids are born. Joe's illness has cost me dearly. The constant stress his illness produces, along with the added burden of not knowing what the next phone call might bring has left me quite fatigued. I have to choose where I can and cannot invest my energy and resources.

A friend once asked what makes having Joe so hard, and it's a question that's difficult to answer. For in working with someone like Joe, one has to suspend the principles of living and functioning as we know them. The internal structures that govern our existence and keep us on track have failed Joe.

Imagine a computer that, because of a massive flaw in its operating system, is unable to perform basic operations. Imagine the frustration of it constantly losing necessary data to yield usable results. Consider how vulnerable that computer would be to crippling viruses without protective software. Think about how exasperating it is when a computer runs slower than it should and even more if it crashes repeatedly. If we use a computer, we have expectations of it. When its performance suffers and there's no way to repair it, it can be quite disruptive.

In many ways, Joe's computer-like brain has a flawed operating system, leaving him unable to accomplish so many tasks most of us take for granted. He either forgets or loses most everything he possesses or needs. He's susceptible to a world that would swallow him up in a heartbeat. He's unreliable, inconsistent, and either takes forever to do the simplest of things or rushes through tasks so that his results are sloppy and unusable. Living in this kind of long-term, discombobulated environment takes a toll on all of us.

Of course, Joe is no computer, he's my precious son, one who loves deeply, forgives quickly, and lives as best he can. I've seen him at his worst, but I've also seen him at his best. I know the quality of his heart. I watch him rise every day, willing to give people another chance no matter how they treated him the day before.

I've heard his heart-felt praise to the God he loves so much, even when he doesn't understand why his life must be so hard. I've seen him run to Georgia's aid when he sensed she was struggling and felt his heart break in response to my own challenges. Along with frustration, my heart grieves this beloved son of mine's suffering.

In addition to these feelings, there's my own constant sense of loss of who Joe could've been. He's missed out on so many accomplishments and milestones most people take for granted. Also long lost is the innocence of life before mental illness and the freedom to live apart from this torment.

I contemplate Joe's future and how that will work out. What will become of Joe after Brian and I are gone? Who will provide the vast amount of support he requires? Will he matter to no one? Will he be too great a burden for Georgia?

There's no laughter that isn't tinged with the exhaustion and heartache of mental illness, no weekend getaway, no grand celebration that isn't colored with his desperate state. I carry this burden everywhere I go and in all I do.

In so many ways, the very task of carrying the burden has been isolating. It's an invisible weight that few people recognize. Fewer still have demonstrated the kind of sensitivity and compassion worthy of my trust. The thing about mental illness is that it's so easy to deny, or perhaps it seems so preventable. But things aren't always as they seem. Mental illness is real. It's taxing. It destroys families, complicates relationships, and depletes resources.

Yet in this valley, a miracle has occurred; not the kind where Joe's been healed of his illness and our troubles are finally over. No, in fact, Joe's fragile state has worsened over the years. The miracle God has chosen to work out, before our very eyes, is the miracle of life and love within these difficulties, even as Joe's flaws continue to rob him of a satisfactory life, of relationships and of a sound mind. Even as the challenges for a brother and sister to choose to honor one another remain great. And even as the gravity of the burden weighs on me. We're finding our way. And we have hope.

The first vacation we took after Joe was diagnosed was difficult. At thirteen years of age, his defiant behavior made it almost impossible to be around him. His madness filled the atmosphere around us so completely, it seemed there was no air to breathe, nowhere to turn for relief, and certainly no pleasure to be had possibly, we feared, ever again.

After several days of mounting tensions and setbacks, we decided to try lunch at a small pizzeria. No sooner had we been seated did Joe start in, ranting on about some random something, I don't even recall what. As he ranted, he became angrier and angrier. We tried everything to calm him down, but to no avail. After the pizzas sat until they were cold,

Brian resorted to sending Joe outside to stand on the walkway so we could finish eating in some semblance of peace.

Of course, it didn't give us peace, because we knew he was suffering. And the mood at our booth was more like the aftermath of war-induced hand-to-hand combat than a fun holiday on the beach. But we had no recourse in dealing with the magnitude of his insanity. I hated it. There are no winners in such a dilemma, only worn and broken souls.

The vacation, something I'd felt our family needed, seemed a total loss. I feared our memories from it would be of the madness, yet an amazing thing happened over time. In the wake of the raging anger and delusional lapses, the memories grew fond. Georgia, who'd been so troubled by Joe's manic episodes she came sobbing to me for comfort, would come to recall laughter, beautiful scenery, and good times.

Brian and I, too, retained good memories of that vacation in spite of the pain, so much that we chose to return to that beach and even the very pizza place we'd been so miserable in for vacations after that. Not only did we discover a vacation destination, we learned there's pleasure in life, even in the face of brokenness.

How we did such a thing was simply answered prayer, and looking in faith for God's provision. Somehow the depth of our love and enjoyment for one another prevailed over the insanity. The reality of faith triumphed over the raging storm. But it wasn't just one vacation. As the years ticked by we continued pursuing help for Joe, all the while trying to preserve the overall well-being of our family. There was no handbook to help us brace for Joe's uncertain future. All we could do was take it a day at a time.

As Joe grew older, it became apparent he wouldn't master the necessary skills to become a licensed driver, but he did have an incredible knack for direction. If he'd been to a place once, no matter where it was located, he could find his way back.

Meanwhile, with Georgia turning sixteen, there was no stopping her from her future. She was sailing through high school and headed for college with opportunities sure to be waiting beyond that. How would Joe, a failing senior in high school, handle the natural progression of Georgia's growing up? It seemed the first real test would be her becoming a licensed driver.

Celebrating this significant birthday of our youngest child, I was excited and proud watching Georgia reach these milestones, but my heart ached for Joe. I felt so helpless thinking of all he was missing out on. The birthday dinner for our new sixteen-year-old was at one of her favorite restaurants. There was no new car for a gift; only a key to my car, which I'd attached to a shiny new key chain along with a new cell phone for her very own.

I worried that watching Georgia receive a key to my car would be hurtful to her brother. Fortunately, Joe usually becomes restless during the course of a meal and often wanders off to relieve his anxiety. Sure enough, as we finished up dinner, he was ready for a break, so while he was gone, we presented Georgia with her gifts. She pocketed the key before he returned, leaving the new phone to show off when he came back. Such a bittersweet moment for all of us; one of so many.

For all of Georgia's strengths, it turns out she wasn't the navigator Joe was. Once she started driving, she discovered how handy it was having Joe around. Together, they formed a precious team as they journeyed through that time period, big brother guiding little sister through the twists and turns of life, if only in that small way.

Over time Georgia gained directional confidence. For good measure, she got an even fancier cell phone with a navigational function built in. Within a year or so, she'd outgrown her need of Joe's help, yet a curious thing happened when Joe was around. She always deferred to his direction, giving him the gift of respect and significance.

All these years later, when Georgia thinks of Joe, she sees a brother who loves her with all his heart. When she hurts, she knows he's moved by her sadness. If she feels mistreated by someone, she knows her big brother longs to make it right. She has a deep appreciation for Joe's ability to continue hoping for and believing the best about people. She loves his resilience and zest for life, his faith in God, and the courage he displays in facing his daily battles.

In Georgia, Joe has developed a deep admiration for her willingness to keep at something in the face of difficulty. He's proud of all she's accomplished, partly because he recognizes accomplishments she takes for granted. I think more than anything, Joe takes pride in the fact that Georgia has grown up to be compassionate toward those who would appear to be undesirable, because it's a quality he's seen so little of in other people. She knows him well and has seen some of his worst behavior, yet she's faithful in loving and respecting him.

As for me, in spite of the difficulties, my heart is full. After such a futile beginning, I've gained a blessed awareness of my Father's delight in me. I can sense His presence in my life and in my circumstances even when those circumstances can feel so hard. This rich knowledge sustains me on a level I didn't even know existed so many years before. In this place of brokenness, God has shown up and worked out something gloriously unimaginable.

In many ways God has brought me full circle. That college roommate who endured my young insecurities has room in her heart for me all these years later, as do others, it turns out. After losing my way at such an early age, God has faithfully helped me find not only myself, but my way home, step by difficult step, faith to ever-increasing faith.

CONCLUSION

Now there is in store for me the crown of
righteousness, which the Lord, the righteous Judge,
will award to me on that day—and not only to me,
but also to all who have longed for his appearing.
PAUL, THE APOSTLE (2 TIMOTHY 4:8)

Our journey, the search for that missing soul, brings
us back to Mt. Olivet. We'll probably need a moment
to collect ourselves, as our time together has
required us to examine much. We're in the presence of the
disciples, and of Jesus Himself, spending His last moments
with these He so dearly loves before He ascends to the
Father.

Standing along a stony pathway beneath a massive fig
tree, Jesus is about to speak. As He opens His mouth, the
disciples are silent, waiting to savor each word that proceeds
from His mouth. There's no lengthy explanation of all that's
transpired over those past forty days since Jesus' crucifixion,
nor is there any frivolous conversation. In this moment

there's a sense of urgency, a sense of these men being desperate to comprehend something, to be moved by something.

Jesus challenges the disciples' about their faith. He calls out their refusal to embrace others within the Body. Talk about a conversation starter. I don't know how they're taking it, but I'm beginning to squirm a bit. I know they love Jesus. I know they trust Him. I've read the stories, but seeing them there . . . that's a perspective changer.

Their response to His words is noteworthy. There's no arguing, no digging their heels into the ground as they try to defend themselves. Looking on, I find myself hoping Jesus will continue speaking. His words are beginning to resonate in my own heart. I can't help but wonder what He's thinking and feeling.

Studying closely, I see the heart of love that His disciples have grown accustomed to, every word spoken, motivated by love. It's so much more than I gathered from just reading through this passage, every word wrapped in genuine affection and compassion.

He understands the challenges. He knows the obstacles they'll encounter because of their faith, but He is also armed with the knowledge that God Himself will sustain them every step of the way. Their God-given faith is far more valuable and finally, more real for them, than anything this present age could throw at them.

Watching the disciples react, I see a measure of trust that takes my breath away. They aren't looking to be coddled. They aren't ready to throw in the towel at Jesus' repeated efforts to pull them toward a prize they can't fully grasp. What is it that compels them to listen and even more, continue receiving Jesus' message? I think it's that unshakable faith that's finally taken hold.

They believe He died for them and that He'll live through them. They're beginning to understand the depth of that truth as well. The sin equation no longer adds up. They don't have to fish and beg and live their lives unfulfilled. They know who they are now, divinely chosen, dearly loved, powerfully enabled; faithfully tended.

The disciples receive Jesus' rebuke with the love and empowering with which it's delivered. And they'll embark on accomplishing a humanly impossible commission--not fulfilling it. Did you notice that distinction? They didn't work to fulfill the Great Commission with busyness and church programs. God fulfilled the commission as they responded to His working in their hearts. This is the way they accomplished their task.

Think about it: with no advanced means of communication, no free Bibles to hand out, no set worship style, no gimmicks or prizes to attract excitement, the disciples shared the story of their new lives, about the all-surpassing power of Christ's redemption and the restoration taking place in their own hearts. And their words did fall on hungry ears with God Himself in their presence. We, as honored time-traveling spectators, know that God grew His church into a divinely connected Body, the one that started with the lives of these very men.

Our family has joined the growing ranks of backyard chicken farmers. The past few springs we were delighted to purchase several newly-hatched chicks. Each batch of peeping chicks needed us to keep them warm, watered, and fed in the safety of our house until they were old enough to survive outside in their pen. A friend then gave us some chickens from her farm that she could no longer keep. We gladly added them to our growing flock. The problem was, one of those hens decided she wanted to be a mama. Real bad.

This cute ball of feathers stopped laying eggs and went broody on us, which is chicken talk meaning she began sitting on a nest of eggs so they would hatch. There was a problem with that, though. The eggs she was sitting on weren't fertile eggs that would grow into baby chicks. Of course, our determined brooder was oblivious to this detail. Day and night she sat as wide and flat as she could, looking more like a plump, feathery pancake than a chicken, so she could keep each individual unfertile egg toasty warm.

Georgia, chief farmhand when home from college, worked with our broody little hen to break her from her trance-like state. But this chicken wouldn't be dissuaded from her mission! Consequently, after Georgia and I entered some serious negotiations with reluctant farmer Brian, we purchased some fertilized eggs for our broody girl to try and hatch.

I had my doubts our earnest hen could endure the rigors of her self-appointed mission, yet for weeks of barely drinking, eating, or even moving, she sat. She even rotated the eggs each day, ever so gently, to provide the environment her babies needed to survive and develop.

And then the incredible happened. After twenty-one days of brooding those fertilized eggs, our hen anxiously presided over eight little foster babies as they began their task of breaking out of their hard shells.

The sounds and movements of those egg shells giving way to tiny beaks pecking furiously for freedom surely gave a weary mama strength to see the task through. Once hatched, wet baby chicks lay in an exhausted heap under the warmth and comfort of their adoring mother. Before long, and with energy restored, eight newborn chicks set out to discover their new world.

After our prior experiences of caring for baby chicks who had no mother, we marveled in fascination as Mama Hazel cared for her babies. She called out to them with sounds we'd never heard a chicken make, clucking and wooing them to eat, to reassure them when they felt threatened, and even to scold them when they wandered too far from her protective eye. Over the course of the next few days, Mama Hazel taught them the skills they'd need to survive their new world. Like adoring fans, her babies took in her every sound and move. Their little worlds revolved around her.

Every day we'd go out to our little nursery to replenish food and water, often bringing extra goodies for mother and growing babies to eat. As the shy babies scattered in eight different directions, Mother would call out, "Cluck, cluck, cluck. Come on over here, youngins; these people are safe and have good food for you to eat."

Each time, after she gave the okay, the babies would come running, eager to see what morsel we'd brought. After a couple of weeks, whenever we'd pay a visit to Hazel and the babies, Hazel would walk right up to us looking for the food she expected us to bring. If she found our hands empty, she'd peck our fingers as if to say, "If you want to come see my babies, you better bring food for them to eat!"

I marveled at Hazel's influence over those chicks. The little things would scurry away at the sight of us, yet they were instantly filled with bravado when Mama called. They'd literally run and jump right into the palm of our hands to indulge in whatever treats we offered at her beckoning.

That's a God-picture, of His protective love for His lost children. It's a reminder that it's Him who fertilizes hearts with holy longing and life. And He longs to trust us with these children, to care for them and feed them wholesome and life-sustaining food.

Without God's Spirit calling out to them, there's no earthly reason for His lost to trust we who call ourselves Christians any more than Hazel's babies trusted Georgia and me. The burden is on Him to woo them in. Our job is to become worthy of His trust by allowing Him to move and grow us along in our own salvation, in the knowledge of His love, in the familiarity of His grace.

God wants us to join in the true labor of Body building, not because He needs us, but because He loves us and wants to bless us. Yet, He knows that we, like the disciples, are growing in a faith that's lacking and incomplete. We're vulnerable to our stubborn pride. And we're susceptible to the distraction of our own best efforts and good intentions. These tendencies cause us to become disconnected from one another, even as we proclaim a Gospel that lacks substance to those in need.

We, like the disciples before us, face a tremendous task in becoming trustworthy sources of nourishment to a starving world and to one another. Can we find the courage to listen and trust as Jesus confronts our faith deficiencies? Can we grasp that time is short and the need is urgent? In the face of all that is familiar, the distractions, misperceptions and evil intentions of a heartless enemy, it's time for love to make a deeper mark in us, for us to be moved deeper in our faith so the glory within us becomes more apparent.

I've seen what can happen to hearts willing to be changed. It was springtime of Joe's senior year of high school. It had been a bad year. We were unsure if Joe would even graduate because of how unstable and hard to manage his behavior had become. Basketball season provided some distraction.

Joe's team handled the beatings they regularly received as well as anyone could expect. However, there was one Christian team Joe came to dread playing because of how mean-spirited they were.

The previous loss to this particular team involved full-court presses being employed against Joe's bewildered team, resulting in turnover after turnover. It wasn't a matter of when Joe's team would score, but if they would score in the ballgame at all. After each turnover and made basket for the opponent, their fans would scream and cheer as if they were winning a state championship.

If one of our boys was fouled, the opposing spectators would howl and chant to disrupt the poor boy's concentration. There was no need, since our guys were definitely no free-throw sharpshooters. Along with the trash-talk, the team's ball-hawking, fancy-crossover dribbling and no-look passing easily stymied our boys' best efforts.

After the game, I observed one of our parents, a nonbeliever, approach the opposing coach. With tears in her eyes, she asked if he'd ever heard of mercy. My heart, already heavy with grief over the disregard they'd shown our boys, groaned with embarrassment at her question. These were, after all, my brothers and sisters in Christ, family I didn't want to be associated with under the circumstances.

Several weeks passed until we were at the end of another winless season. Brian, Georgia, and I prepared to cheer Joe on for what would be the last conference tournament of his high school career. His game was early that Saturday in what would be a long day of basketball, with a champion to be crowned during the final game that night.

Unfortunately, Joe's team had drawn this same dreaded opponent from earlier in the season. By virtue of their season records, they were scheduled to play in a non-advancing game where the winner would merely be recognized in the final standings. Joe and his teammates arrived at the gym and were somehow excited even as we parents braced for what would surely be another cruel beating.

Surprisingly, after an entire season of missed tip-offs, there was Joe, our team's center, with his fingertips on the basketball. Though he was the tallest on the team, his jumping skills were lacking, so his making contact with the ball was an unusual sight. For a moment I held my breath thinking he'd won his first tip-off, but then he tipped it to the opposing team. Still, this was a victory, however small.

As the game wore on, I noticed the opponents didn't bother with their flashy moves. Also different, they didn't employ their usual suffocating defense. To all of us parents' amazement and delight, our guys were actually being competitive. As I surveyed the situation, it began to dawn on me what was happening. The opposing players, whose faces had become pretty familiar over the years, were playing out of position. Their big guys who normally played around the basketball goal were playing the guard positions, and the guys who normally played as guards were playing down around the basket.

As the game progressed, Joe and his teammates were gaining confidence and taking better care of the basketball. It seemed everyone on our team was hitting shots. Though outscored in the first quarter, we came roaring back in the second. We were able to build a small lead by the third period. When the fourth quarter came around, we found ourselves still ahead. But we were unaccustomed to this kind of success and began to suffer some serious lapses as our opponent made a furious comeback.

In the last seconds of regulation, they tied the game to set up overtime. We parents, along with the coach, let out a collective groan. How would our kids deal with their very first overtime period? After another four minutes were played out, the scoreboard read 62 – 56, in favor of our boys! These were more points than our team scored in any one game since my son had been playing on the team.

That, however, wasn't the real story. As I watched the game, I realized something larger than life was happening. For our team, even when the game became tight near the end, our better players continued involving the rest of their teammates. They cared more that their teammates who rarely scored had a chance at feeling successful than for winning the game. By the time it was over, ten players' names from our team were entered into the scorebook, an unheard of accomplishment for our challenged team. However, their commitment to this task, along with the sharp play of the opposing team, cost us a comfortable lead.

The other team had been up to something as well. Even with the game on the line, they stuck to their game plan. They played solid defense, though not aggressive defense. They took good shots. But since their young men were playing positions they were unaccustomed to playing, they made mistakes they generally wouldn't have made. I noticed several of the opponents' eyes light up ever so subtly from time to time, and it occurred to me they were experiencing success in ways that were new to them, too. But unlike our previous games together, they didn't gloat nor boast at any time during the game.

What happened that made this game so different? The opposing team chose to approach this game differently, yet they attempted to do it without drawing attention to this fact. To give our guys a chance to compete, they merely leveled the playing field. They didn't give the game away, which would've felt demeaning to our guys. They found a way to honor our boys by playing unfamiliar positions, and in so doing, chose the more noble goal.

By game's end, our coach was in tears. Our parents were in tears. And amazingly, there wasn't a loser to be found. Our guys were elated with the success they'd experienced. They rebounded, made shots, took care of the basketball, took care of their teammates, and on top of that, they didn't lose. The opposing team's players, their parents, and their coaches came and congratulated our guys, and told them how great they played.

If our guys played well, how can I characterize how our opponent played? These guys demonstrated that being Christlike means approaching opportunities differently, not by putting forth the name of God or a set of ideals, but by making themselves available for God to change. And at least for that day, He did. He changed their routine, took them out of their comfort zones, and changed their way of seeing things.

And they submitted to spreading the Gospel in this way, by playing positions they were unaccustomed to playing, one that required different skills than were their strong suit. They did it by reflecting in their actions that a heart is worth more than a contest. In doing so, it placed them within God's desire to accomplish something much more precious than a good stat line, the same truth the Apostle Paul discovered so long ago; that in our weakness, God is strong.

By day's end, the championship game of the conference was coming to an end. Both of those contenders were talented and deserving. It was a good game, each team playing hard until the winner was decided. But what a different kind of ending. That championship game had a winner and a loser. It paled in comparison to that earlier game, the one leading to a measly seventh-place finish.

For me, the seventh-place game was the game of a lifetime. Those young men displayed the courage to change, becoming true champions in our midst. And the parent who'd earlier asked about mercy experienced mercy in a profound and moving way.

How does that translate for us? There's no publishable blue-print, other than the aid of His written word. There's only each of us choosing moment by moment to step outside ourselves, outside our comfort zones, and outside our realm of past and present experiences to embrace a God whose navigational instincts are far different than we've probably imagined, and whose purposes are more worthy than the best of our intentions.

We have the opportunity to step into our life's greatest work, the working out of our salvation, to grow more empowered through the process of grace. The dignity of this work stands higher than any earthly merit, and the result far exceeds our mind's capacity to envision. Now is the time to participate in this work. Now is the time to take hold of our rightful place in one connected Body of Christ, a heart at a time. The only sacrifice required is our brokenness.

Duty calls, and our time here on Mt. Olivet is coming to an end. We've seen how the disciples welcomed Jesus into every aspect of their broken lives, how they loved His appearing, even when His words challenged, even when they were exposed.

And now it's our turn. There, in His presence, Jesus' eyes come to rest on each of us, loving us, knowing our pain, our fears, and our struggles. Filled with compassion, He begins to speak. Oh that we'll display the same courage as Peter, John, and the rest of the disciples. And like others through the generations, including an unlikely basketball team that gained my respect, may we join together to listen and keep seeing, Jesus.

The End

EIDŌ LOGOS

(TO PERCEIVE THE WORD)

God spoke the world into existence, man into being. This is an amazing fact. He spoke words, and the very thing He intended, happened. But since that time words have undergone a steady barrage of arrows.

They've ebbed and flowed as the generations of man have made use of them. And they've become marred by an enemy who fears our grasp of them. Words as we know and understand them can be watered-down, overused, underused, misinterpreted, misspoken, and withheld completely.

Then there are words we've come to think of as religious words. These words have endured an especially fierce assault. What secrets do they hold that the enemy would seek to distort or conceal their meaning? What possibilities exist beyond the religious associations that often rob them of their beauty?

What if we were to reconsider our perception of divinely inspired words, to grasp a better understanding with the eyes of our heart? Because followers of Christ have a heritage. We have a quality of life to possess and a glory just waiting to be discovered. Even more, we have a God to know. And we can embark on this great journey, with God's help, one word at a time!

The definitions to follow aren't definitions per se, but merely thoughts to ponder.

be•com•ing
beginning to be; a process of change; developing capabilities and possibilities

bod•y of Christ
one unit made up of distinctive people professing the same God, including servants, laborers, and ministers, each of whom have different giftings

faith
grasping and holding onto the reality of things inspired by the Spirit but that remain unseen

found
to see and discover for one's self; to gain understanding

glo•ry
in God: highly renowned; completely magnificent; His character distinguished and worthy; in Him there is dignity and grace; in man, the evidence of God living within one's heart

grace
holy empowering influence that turns man to God; then it keeps him, strengthening and increasing his faith,

knowledge, and affection; an enabling to do what God calls one to do

lost
to become useless or defeated; to be damaged; to experience an inability to be fully alive either emotionally, physically, or spiritually

love
a reaction to the experience of being loved by God; turning toward, being mindful of, accepting; embracing

mer•cy
a never-ending gift of compassion and loyalty; freedom from condemnation

per•fect
a process that's brought to its end; becoming complete; transforming/not conforming: the difference? To be transformed is to become, to take on another form; to conform is to act; to be similar to

prayer
a coming together of the minds; communication, revelation

re•deem
the act of finding, returning, or restoring; to feel one's self again; to liberate from the power of another by payment or ransom

sal•va•tion
the sum of the benefits and blessings made available for believers in Christ to discover as they're transformed

sanc•tif•i•ca•tion
the effect of becoming holy; working out one's salvation

tes•ti•mo•ny/wit•ness
to confirm what has been divinely revealed or inspired

WORKS CITED

CHAPTER ONE

1. Blue Letter Bible. "Gospel of Mark 16:14 - (NIV - New International Version)." Blue Letter Bible. 1996-2012. 2 Oct 2012. <http://www.blueletterbible.org/Bible.cfm?b=Mar&c=16&t=NIV >.

CHAPTER TWO

1. Gesenius, Heinrich Friedrich Wilhelm. Gesenius's Hebrew and Chaldee Lexicon to the Old Testament Scriptures. Edited by S. P. Tregelles. Blue Letter Bible. 1857. 26 October 2010. <http://www.blueletterbible.org/lang/lexicon/lexicon. cfm?Strongs=H5414&t=KJV>.

CHAPTER THREE

1. Invictus. Dir. Clint Eastwood. With Morgan Freeman and Matt Damon. Warner Brothers, 2009.

2. Metcalfe, Luke. People Statistics>Population by Country. (2003-2008): Internet. http://www.nationmaster.com/graph/peo_pop-people population August 28, 2008.

3. National Crime Victims Research and Treatment Center, Medical University of South Carolina. "Victim Reactions to Traumatic Events Handout" January 25, 2011.
<http://www.musc.edu/ncvc/resources_public/ victim_reactions_general_trauma.pdf>.

CHAPTER FOUR

1. Montell, William L. Singing the Glory Down: Amateur Gospel Music in Southcentral Kentucky 1900-1990. Lexington: The University Press of Kentucky, 1991.

CHAPTER SEVEN

1. DeYoung, Donald B. "What's Special About the Sea of Galilee?" Christian Answers Network Web. 4 May 2011. Christian Answers Network. 1992.
<http://www.christiananswers.net/q-eden/ednk-seaofgalilee.html>.

2. Matthew 14:27, The Amplified Bible.

CHAPTER EIGHT

1. Eighteenth-century English Proverb, "Thomas Fuller, Gnomologia (1732)" Dictionary.com. 8 May 2011. Columbia University Press. 1996
http://quotes.dictionary.com/A_blind_man_will_not_thank_you_for>.

CHAPTER NINE

1. "What happened to the 12 disciples of Jesus?" Reasonable Faith: Rational Evidences for Christ Jesus . 7 June 2011. Ichthus.
<http://www.ichthus.info/Disciples/intro.html>.

CHAPTER ELEVEN

1. Yancey, Philip. "Denominational Diagnostics." Christianity Today. 30 Aug. 2011. Christianity Today International. 27 Nov. 2008.
<http://www.christianitytoday.com/ct/2008/ november/27.119.html>.

2. Blue Letter Bible. "Gospel of Luke 9 - (KJV - King James Version)." Blue Letter Bible. 1996-2011. 30 Aug 2011. <http://www.blueletterbible.org/Bible.cfm?b=Luk&c=9&t=KJV>.

ABOUT THE AUTHOR

Carrie Bullock Fisher is an author and teacher. She is the founder of Looking Glass Stories, a publishing and teaching ministry devoted to encouraging followers of Christ in the ongoing work of restoration and transformation.

She lives near Nashville, Tennessee with her husband, Brian. They, along with two children Joe and Georgia, have spent the past two decades+ restoring their 210-year-old home.

She enjoys cooking, hiking with her dogs, cheering on her favorite sports teams, and taking care of her chickens out back.

You may contact Carrie about speaking and teaching engagements at:

Looking Glass Stories
URL: http://lookingglassstories.com
E-Mail: carrie@lookingglassstories.com

Made in the USA
Charleston, SC
19 December 2012